CHEDDAR GORGE

CONTENTS

I.

INTRODUCTION

ENGLISH CHEESES

I.—INTRODUCTION

By Sir John Squire

This book arose out of a correspondence in *The Times* at the end of 1935 and the beginning of 1936. M. Th. Rousseau, a French connoisseur, wrote to complain that when he visited England he could not get Stilton—the waiters said it was out of season. Many people wrote to explain that perhaps it was out of season, and that in most decent London restaurants Stilton, when in condition, could be obtained, if only after pressure. But the correspondence did attract attention to the neglect of English cheese generally, and to the gradual attrition of English cheeses by foreign invasion and native indifference and ignorance.

Now, no citizen of the world would wish to decry foreign cheeses, or foreign food either. As I write these lines I have just come back from a holiday in the mountains above Lake Como (staying with Italian friends, spaghetti, cheese and wine). In order to get to my destination I had to go to Como, which has silks and a lovely Cathedral, and wait for two hours in an out-of-doors café within sight of the pier. Lunch, as it was noon, was indicated, and I sat down, after two years' absence from the Continent, metaphorically tucking a napkin into my neck below a non-existent beard, and looking forward to a really Italian table d'hôte, with all the dishes lingering on mind and tongue, with languishing vowels.

11

What did I find ? Apparently they had become resigned to the coarser kind of German, American and English visitors, who haven't the sense to adapt their food to climate or surroundings. " Coelum non animam mutant " : the sky may change but the set rules and regulations about filling the stomach do not.

The first course, as it were hors d'œuvres, consisted of eggs and bacon ; and that at lunch-time, under a baking noon and an Italian sky, with blue lake and mountains all around. The second was " Mixed Grill " ; and there was a great deal to follow. The mixed grill contained liver, bacon, kidneys and sausages, and was accompanied by thick fingers of fried potatoes. Fat women and young men were eating them all around me, terrified, apparently, lest they should shrivel. I ordered an omelette and a bottle of white Italian wine, and tried to keep my eyes off all those gluttons. Just as I was finishing with cheese, a tall thin Englishman and a flat-chested wife, wiping their brows, came and sat down at the next table to me ; they looked at the menu and the beads multiplied on their brows. I couldn't help speaking. I said : " Excuse me, sir, but I expect you find the lunch too much for you."

" I should think I do, in this climate," he replied.

" If I may say so," I went on, " you'd better follow my example and have an omelette, with perhaps a little fruit to follow." He grunted assent and did so.

But he wasn't really a citizen of the world. No sooner had he stopped grumbling about these foreigners supplying us with hot sausages at an Italian August lunch (and the supply simply must have responded to a demand) than he began complaining about the surroundings. A little rusty tram clattered by. " Look at that tram," he exclaimed to his

12

dutiful wife, " absolutely filthy. I consider it a disgrace to a place like this." The word " insular " rose, unspoken, to my lips.

And the word " insular " cuts both ways. Most English people, living on this island, away from the Continent and full of compromises, will regard foreigners as strange beasts. Walking in Devonshire the other day, and talking in a country ale-house with a landlord who kept cows and poultry, I heard him sum up the world situation in these terms : " Zur, there bain't no country but this." I had heard the sentiment often enough before ; it spreads like a rash whenever them vurriners appear to be fighting one another all about nothing. But the insularity works another way, too ; them vurriners are as marvellous as they are mischievous and unaccountable and incomprehensible. They can make, in their absurd way, music, art, and cheese as we cannot. The result is that Miss Smith and Miss Jones, admirable ballet-dancers, have to appear in the Russian ballet as Smithova and Jonesova ; that Mr. Robinson, the great tenor, appears as Signor Robinello ; and that English cheese is without honour in its own country and amongst its own kin. Consequently it is without honour abroad. If we don't celebrate it both at home and abroad, it will cease to be. The world will be the poorer. Our entertainment to visitors will be feebler. Couldn't one give one's French friends a better welcome were one able to say, " Come down to Dorset with me and we'll taste the local cheese! " Do they really want to go to Dorchester to be given a choice of Gorgonzola or Camembert ?

There are few parts of England which do not remember cheeses extinct or nearly extinct. Not all of them, I dare say, deserve resuscitation; the evidence suggests, for instance, that the man who ate Suffolk cheese might just as well have been

13

"MIGHT JUST AS WELL HAVE BEEN EATING OLD MOTOR TYRES."

eating old motor tyres. But it was possible a century ago to travel throughout England and sample local cheeses everywhere. To-day most of them are unobtainable unless in small quantities from eclectic merchants. Even in first-class chophouses the only English cheeses on offer will be Stilton, Cheddar or Cheshire; in most places only Cheddar and Cheshire, more likely than not American. Gorgonzola (often, even before sanctions, made in Denmark) is more familiar to many English people than any English cheese; and such a notable cheese as Double Gloucester is known to few but epicures.

No sensible person would wish to exclude or decry foreign cheeses. It would be a calamity were no more Camembert, Brie or Bel Paese to land on these shores: Dutch cheese is a change and Parmesan is a necessary of life. But it is ridiculous

14

that we should neglect our own fine cheeses to such an extent that a foreigner can visit these shores (Europe in fact knows as little of our cheese as it does of our landscape-painting) without discovering that we possess any, let alone thinking of importing some to his own country. Taste can only be improved and cheese-makers heartened if those who care for England, Cheese, and Farming, indulge in vigorous propaganda. Supply will only come from demand, and there will be no demand unless the public is stirred from its present apathy and brought to realise the mechanical monotony of its present diet.

The causes of our present lack of pride in home produce and interest in the subtleties of the palate may be left to others to trace. Puritanism and Utilitarianism I dare say may be partly responsible; each despising art and taste. The neglect of cheese, at any rate, is no new thing: it is forty years since Mrs. Roundell, in one of the finest, amplest and best written Cookery Books ever published, said sorrowfully: " Some persons, however, still have the courage to enjoy cheese." Unless more acquire this well-rewarded courage it is likely

"CAN'T WE EVEN TALK ABOUT THE CHEESE?"

that all our English cheeses will die out and that we shall end with a few European cheeses for the intelligent minority (for cheese in France and Italy will not die) and for the others mere generic soapy, tasteless stuff, white or red, called cheese, imported from across the Atlantic. The appetite may grow by what it feeds on : it may also diminish : another generation and our population may positively dislike the strong ripe cheeses of our fathers.

Of the chapters in this book all except two deal exclusively with English cheeses ; those two are occupied with Scotch Dunlop and with Irish cheeses as a salute to neighbouring kingdoms. Many cheeses might have been added—such as Double Cottenham (made now only in a few farmhouses), the cheeses of Derby and Lancashire, and the various cream cheeses. But the book had to have limits.

The references to Canadian and other American cheeses are intended only to apply to the bulk of that which we import from North America ; it is a scandal that names like Cheddar and Cheshire should be allowed to apply to the stuff. I have heard of, though never tasted, several American cheeses said to be individual and good, such as Rowland, Wisconsin, Redskin, Golden Buck and O.K.A., said to be made by Trappist Fathers. If these be good and will travel, by all means let us try some ; there cannot be too many good cheeses within our reach. But at present it is English cheese that is most in need of trumpeting, just as it is the Roast Beef of Old England and not the Roast Lamb of New Zealand— which latter, by the way, some tuneful New Zealander ought by now to have gratefully celebrated in song.

(May I add, as a postcript, that I must not be held responsible for those of my colleagues who have called a Welsh Rabbit a "rarebit"—a vile modern refinement.)

II.
STILTON

II.—STILTON

By Sir John Squire

Hotspur, in Shakespeare, exasperated by the timid, tedious, superstitious Glendower, exclaims of him :

> I had rather live
> With cheese and garlick in a windmill, far,
> Than feed on cates and have him talk to me
> In any summer house in Christendom.

Here, the hero, unlike Horace who was happy to write

> Me pascunt olivae
> Me cichorea levesque malvae

appears to regard the Simple Life as merely the less unpleasant of two gross evils : though as concerns the one matter of garlic Horace would certainly agree with him, as is indicated in the third Epode where he laments " quid hoc veneni saevit in praecordiis " and prays that Maecenas, who had given it to him, should suffer the worst of fates if the offence were repeated. Mr. Belloc, perhaps, would more thoroughly accept what Hotspur contemned : he possesses a windmill and he has written notably about cheese and the eating of raw onions.

It is possible that one could live on that diet ; Mr. Burdett in his *Little Book of Cheese* quotes the old Doctor Thomas Muffett : Was not that a great cheese, think you, wherewith Zoro-

"LIVED IN THE WILDERNESS TWENTY YEARS . . . WITHOUT ANY OTHER MEAT."

aster lived in the wilderness twenty years together without any other Meat ?

and calculates that the cheese, to last, must have weighed a ton and a half. Remembering the widow's cruse of the other Prophet, it may be that Zoroaster had technical resources which obviated the necessity of so great a bulk. But supposing a man were to wish to live on cheese alone, and that it were possible, there is no cheese in the world so nourishing and so little likely to pall as Stilton. Everybody who has ever entertained a Stilton must remember the sigh of sorrow which goes up when the last of it has been eaten or has become inedibly dry.

It is the King of Cheeses, if all the qualities of cheeses are taken into account : that a cheese should be not only a " thing in itself "[1] (to use the phrase of German philosophers who

[1] Ding an sich

22

thought that green cheese was what the moon was made of) and as the perfect rounding off of a meal—the sunset of it, caseus et praeterea nihil—but as, at need, a meal in itself. There are excellent cheeses which can agreeably be daubed on the remains of a roll at the end of luncheon, without adding noticeably to the amount consumed ; and some of them are hardly distinguishable from the butter with which they are usually taken. But the best of the creamy and semi-liquid kinds need accessories, can only be eaten in small quantities, and cannot be conceived of as staples of life. One cannot imagine Zoroaster, whatever his magic antidotes against time and clime, spending twenty years of solitude in the unmitigated company of a mound of "Cream" or of Camembert— before a day was out he would have been thinking more of the Camembert's crust or even the other's silver paper as something approximating to solid food than he would have thought of the softness within. On the other hand there are solid, leathery or rubbery cheeses which are undoubtedly edible in quantities on occasion but which are either so tame or so peculiar that they would become rapidly wearisome. And, again, there are sturdy cheeses so pungent and even stinging that a little of them taken "neat" must go a long way. Ripe Stilton, as an unaccompanied iron ration, would excel them all. And, as the conclusion of a meal, it should always be regarded as a full-sized course in itself, and not as a trimming ; and thought should be taken beforehand accordingly. To begin a meal with hors d'œuvres which is going to end with Stilton is not to whet but to waste the appetite —olives I don't count.

When Stilton began it is evident no man knows. The process of making it was doubtless a gradual growth. A recent correspondence in *The Times* showed an almost acrimonious difference of opinion as to where the credit of its invention lies. Had it not been for the fact that the French have recently erected a statue to Madame Harel, the inventress of Camembert, people would hardly have expected a precise name and date; many writers consoled themselves with the reflection that they know where and when and by whom it was first put upon the general market. In the eighteenth century it is reputed to have been made at Quenby Hall, in Leicestershire, and to have been known there as Lady Beaumont's cheese, or, as some say, Mrs. Ashby's; and, after, the Quenby housekeeper is said to have married a farmer at Dalby, whence, via a daughter, Mrs. Paulet, it reached Stilton, where it was sold at the Bell by Cooper Thornhill, Mrs. Paulet's kinsman. This is the generally accepted story and it is certain that from the late eighteenth century onwards it was customarily sold outside the Bell to coach-passengers and others going along the Great North Road. No more suitable market-place (though it be not its birthplace) could have been devised for it than the village of Stilton and the Bell Inn. Even the " fumum et opes strepitumque " of the Great North Road to-day has not destroyed the peace of that wide old village street with its long stone Tudor inn with the great hanging gold sign of the Bell; and the local market, which presumably was killed by the temporary desertion of the roads during the railway era, might well be revived now. But the theory that, in the words of Mr. Osbert Burdett, " it was first sold in the last decade of the eighteenth century by its inventor's (Mrs. Paulet) kinsman " can be killed by a couplet. Both the cheese and the name for it go back at least two generations farther. In Pope's Imitations of Horace appear these lines in the course of a reference to Prior's story of the town mouse and the country mouse:

24

THE "BELL" AT STILTON.

25   D

Cheese, such as men in Suffolk make,
But wish'd it Stilton for his sake.

This takes Stilton, so-named, back to George II.'s days ; not only that, but it holds it up as the ne plus ultra of cheeses as contrasted to the lumpish stuff from Suffolk. And further, since Pope referred to it, who seldom moved from Twickenham and the south, it is at least probable that Stilton was at that time on sale in London, and well known there. Research might well produce earlier allusions. If readers will produce such they will be incorporated in later editions.[1] Mrs. Paulet, however, would not have got her reputation for nothing ; and she deserves her statue for having put Stilton " on the map " as nobody before her seems to have done.

Stilton holds its own. Cheddar and Cheshire are in difficulties, though they may struggle back. When those of us who are now in middle life were young these were the stock English cheeses in all English households and inns. If you stopped, on a summer walk, for luncheon at the Cross Keys or the Mariner's Rest you had a pint of bitter, English Cheddar (probably) or Cheshire (possibly) and newish bread with inviting crust : to-day you are usually fobbed off with so-called Cheddar, like mild soap, from across the Atlantic, or so-called Cheshire, like clay coloured with marigolds, also from across the Atlantic. The rage for cheapness is one cause. The scandalous lack of protection for English commodity-names (why *should* a thing be sold as Cheddar when it isn't?) is another. The invention of the bicycle is another ; when one was young the ordinary labourer had his meal of bread and good cheese and good beer or cider out of a stone jar under the hedge, whereas to-day he rides back to his cottage and is

[1] We should also like information as to the legend that, long ago, Cheddar was ripened in caves, as is Roquefort.

"HAD HIS MEAL OF BREAD AND GOOD CHEESE AND GOOD
BEER . . . UNDER THE HEDGE."

given by his wife salmon or corned beef out of a tin. Stilton, however, was rather a luxury; the rich like it; it is just possible that there would be a row if bogus Stilton were put upon the market after the fashion of bogus Gorgonzola; and in any event no plausible substitute for it, inferior or otherwise, has been invented. The sales of Stilton in recent years have increased; and if, as seems likely, more attention in the near future is devoted to food and drink (middle-class Puritanism with its gross feeding and its hatred of refinement being on the wane) they are likely to increase.

Demand is not likely to outrun supply. The character of Stilton is determined by the milk of which it is made, and that upon the grass which the cows eat, and that upon the soil; and Stilton is not one of those products like genuine Chianti or Imperial Tokay which are only themselves if they come from a particular patch of a few acres. The pastures on which it thrives are widespread in Huntingdonshire, Notts, Leicestershire and Rutland; and some first-class Stiltons nowadays come from Derbyshire—which also, like Leicestershire, has its own peculiar cheese, though little of it is now made. As with all cheeses of wide consumption the manufacture of Stilton is now largely carried on in company-owned factories, though there are still flourishing dairies whose owners carry on with their own milk and that of neighbouring farmers. The cheeses of these latter are often among the best: for that matter there are old village wives who can make magnificent cheeses by rule of thumb or no apparent rule while scientifically trained girls freshly armed from college with thermometers, percentages and other gadgets may fail hopelessly—cheese-making is an art rather than a science.

The summer and early autumn months are the best season for making cheese, Stilton included. In those months the

MAKING STILTON CHEESE.

milk is naturally richest ; later the grass wanes (winter foods
—cotton-cake and such—are no adequate substitute) and then
come the frosts. The cheeses take anything up to six months
to ripen ; it follows that the best time for eating them runs
roughly from November to April. I made this statement in
print once, and a man wrote to tell me that he had once had
perfect Stilton on a hot August day in a Great Western Railway
restaurant—perhaps that Lucullan paradise which has delighted

so many gourmets in the station at Bristol. He was, he admitted, bewildered, and asked how the miracle had been achieved. The answer was a refrigerator. It sounds very odd to me. Anyhow I should no more want Stilton on a hot August day than I should want boiled silverside and dumplings ; Stilton is essentially a thing for the cold months, when appetites are robust and in want of warming up : and nothing is as good out of season as in, even if you can get it.

The old method of starting fermentation was to mix the morning's milk with the previous evening's which had acquired a slight tincture of sourness. To-day a " starter " is universally used in the form of lactic acid bacteria procured from the Ministry of Agriculture. The milk is heated to a required temperature and then rennet—the operation of which is familiar to any one who has ever made junket—is added, which separates the curd from the whey. The curd is strained off, salt is added in the proportion of one to three or four, and the mixture is put into a wooden frame, of a Stilton's familiar shape and size, in which, aided by frequent turning, it gets rid of more whey. After a week or so it is put into a cloth wrapping which absorbs more moisture; after another week or so, the surface being now quite dry, the young Stilton emerges. Another week in coolness and damp and its characteristic grey rind is formed. Now, about a month after the beginning of the making the slow process of maturing sets in, which may take six months.

If it is allowed to be completed, that is. Large-scale manufacturers and retailers alike, because of the expense of cellarage and the desire for a quick turn-over, are delighted to get rid of their cheese as early as they can ; and a great deal of Stilton, not to mention other cheeses, is eaten when it is much too young. It is the commonest thing to be offered in hostelries

30

and chop-houses Stilton which is still hard, white, chalky and, to the taste, rather acid, and one frequently hears waiters warning their favourite customers that " the Stilton is not quite ripe yet, sir "—as though there were any sense in cutting it before it is ripe. But what the temptations to retailers are, what the difficulties of very small and very busy dealers, what the care, labour and expense involved in the perfect nursing and marketing of Stilton may easily be realised by any one who goes over the vaults of a great and scrupulous cheese-monger.

I may take, as an instance, Messrs. Fortnum and Mason, whose sales of Stilton are very large, as befits such notable specialists in English cheeses in general. The privileged visitor is taken underground by a lift and finds himself in a series of beautifully clean cellars (blue-washed because flies do not like blue) full of cheeses and sides and hams—cellars are necessary for the storage of cheeses as they will mature properly only in darkness and an even cool temperature. Various rooms are crossed, one's guide turning on switches as he goes, until at last one reaches the Stiltons which, as befits their dignity, have a chapel to themselves, full of shelves and turning implements. There they stand in rows, scores of them, some in cloths, some unbound. Every other day they are turned in order that the curd should retain an even consistency, and every single day they are brushed in order to keep them clear of mites—for these creatures bore inwards and are not, as people think, spontaneously generated by cheese any more than (pace Shakespeare) the sun actually breeds maggots. The job is one in which a man should take as much pride as a groundsman takes in his wicket at Lord's.

He who purchases cheese from an establishment like that may be certain that he will get something ready for eating:

though even among the customers of the best retailers there is some difference of taste regarding the prime of cheeses, and there are even people so eccentric, or so uneducated, that they actually prefer Stilton immature, chalky and sour. These may find what they want anywhere; they may even buy it in flat segments in London bars. But for the purchaser in general, who goes to a local shop which stocks Stilton and likes to see it for himself or herself, this much may be said. The cheese should be creamy, not white; the blue mould should be well distributed; and cracks should not be conspicuous. A little brown around the edges is normal when the cheese is mature; patches of brown elsewhere mean imperfect grass. Tasting is always advisable; the cheese-trier leaves little trace behind it.

A Stilton should be cut before it is over-ripe; it should be finished before it is dry. The custom is now common of slicing it horizontally so as to expose the least possible extent of surface to drying. This way the last of the cheese will be moister; but nobody will ever get the heart of the cheese as one gets it from the middle with a scoop, which latter in the end leaves one with a desiccated husk. Each must choose for himself; in any event a cheese will not go bone-dry if you eat it fast enough.

And why not do so? More than one reason is advanced as to why the modern small household shrinks from Stilton: and it is certainly true that the presence of a Stilton in a very bijou flat may make itself disagreeably felt, particularly if the weather turns warm. But there is no reason why a household of even two should (though, unassisted, they will hardly dispose of a whole Stilton before it dries) cope with a half Stilton in the period between its prime and its decay—in fact I have had recent proof of this—provided it is regarded as something more than a trimming. And it should be eaten nearly mature.

There are cheeses so mild that they need help; cheeses so strong that they need toning down. I have seen in commercial hotels people chopping up Canadian " Cheddar " and adding Yorkshire Relish to it; and it is common and pardonable for men who are eating the powerful produce of Gorgonzola to mitigate it with cucumber or raw tomato in addition to butter. But mature Stilton needs neither modification nor mollification. The delicacy of crisp celery is permissible with it, particularly if one is making a breakfast of it. But butter does not help it; it has salt enough of its own; and all that it needs for accompaniment is bread, not too stale.

It is an insult to this cheese to buy or sell it by the pound. It is not a compliment to buy or sell portions of it in little jars. The best merchants know this; they merely shrug their shoulders and say that the demand must be met by the supply. The only hope therefore is that of educating the public taste which, in the last fifty years, has been steadily vitiated through a number of obvious causes. And if we can only cultivate an appreciation of and belief in our own cheeses we may recover some of those which we have lost and even lead foreigners to respect them. It is impossible to travel in France without encountering a great diversity of local cheeses as well as those of general fame, from Normandy to Alsace and so to the South, and in varying degrees this is true of all Western countries, Spain being perhaps the most deficient. Some of the most delightful foreign cheeses—including the finest of the soft Swiss ones—will not travel. But we may be fairly sure that any really good and keepable foreign cheese has its chances in England, and it is likely that in the best London clubs and hotels there is more cheese from France alone—Roquefort, Port Salut, Camembert and Brie—annually consumed than there is of all the English cheeses put together. Variety is a good thing and a good cheese is welcome from whencesoever it comes : few of us would wish to be Zoroaster. But it is scandalous that every British household should be familiar with, say, Edam (the round Dutch redskins) but that hardly anybody on the Continent has ever heard of any English cheese at all.

A little Stilton used to be exported to Germany ; beyond that I do not know that any English cheese has ever gone abroad in noticeable quantities excepting only Cheshire, which is widely known as Chester. I was first apprised of this before the War by a Hungarian friend. He was telling me that he had been attending a debate of the Hungarian Parliament. A deputy had begun a sentence with " As the English writer Chesterton says . . ." when he was fiercely interrupted by a colleague who leapt up and shouted : " Chesterton is a cheese! " If our agricultural industry were not so depressed and the Ministry of Agriculture were able to be as active in promoting the export of English cheese as its sister department is in importing foreign dairy products in exchange for coal, the world, which does not know as yet that we have great painters, might at least learn that we have great cheeses. Stilton, at least, should be obtainable in every good hotel in Northern and Central Europe and, before it can be obtainable, its virtues must be made widely known by propaganda amongst foreigners. Tens of thousands of them swarm into London every year. How many of them, at the "Magnifique " and the " Superbe," are ever pressed to attempt Stilton? Why, half the waiters have never heard of it!

Throughout the nineteenth century British authors paid frequent tribute to Stilton, though there are always those who prefer to show their connoisseurship by mentioning something outlandish. In Jane Austen's *Emma* there is a reference to Stilton. Emma, out for a walk, had hung behind Harriet and Mr. Elton in the hope of giving them a chance of tender passages. At last they looked round and she was obliged to join them :

Mr. Elton was still talking, still engaged in some interesting detail ; and Emma experienced some disappointment when she found that he was only giving his fair companion an account of yesterday's party at his friend Cole's, and that she was come in herself for the Stilton cheese, and the North Wiltshire, the butter, the celery, the beetroot, and all the dessert.

" This would soon have led to something better, of course," was her consoling reflection, " anything interests between those who love ; and anything will serve as an introduction to what is near the heart."

But it may be that Harriet, who had already been described as not clever, did not respond to the Stilton ; which may explain why the course of this love did not run smooth, or even at all. Mary Lamb was very fond of Stilton and there is a letter in which Charles thanks Thomas Allsop for sending them " the best I ever tasted . . . the delicatest, rainbow-hued, melting piece I ever flavoured." Stilton ought to have been mentioned in " Handley Cross," and I thought it was. Looking back I can only find references to " chopped cheese " (toasted?) at the Hunt Dinner and the cheese " strong, soft and leathery " to which Mr. Jorrocks helped himself too greedily at that awful repast at the Muleygrubs. Elsewhere he is recorded as having written : " P.S.2. Tell Fortnum and

35

Mazon to send me dozen pots of marmeylad," so his knowledge of the right cheese must be assumed.

    .   .   .   .

As to what is to be drunk with Stilton is a matter of taste, a matter also of what one has eaten and drunk before it has been reached. There are those who eat liquor with it, as it were, pouring port or beer upon it after it has gone dry. Moistening no doubt: but the Stilton may still cry " Non sum qualis eram." Beer or burgundy, to my thinking ; but better still, water, and whatever you like afterwards.

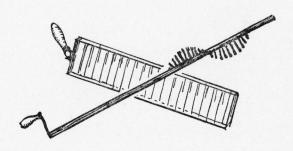

III.
INTERLUDE BY THE ARTIST

III.—INTERLUDE BY THE ARTIST

By Ernest H. Shepard

Having climbed the hill at Randwich, I expected to see a pleasant old-world village—a suitable setting for the once famous cheese fair—but all I found was a straggling line of cottages, a small Inn and a half-developed garage. It was a grand situation on the top side of the hill and could boast a fine view, with Stroud lying below in the valley. A hot, sleepy Sunday morning had sent people indoors, but I found an old man nailing up his trellis by the front door and asked him if he could help me. " There baint no cheese fair round 'ere. Maybe there used to be, but I ain't ne'er 'eard tell o' 'un. They doant make no cheese, eyther. You'm 'ave to go Chipping Sodbury way for that," he added. So I turned my back on Randwich and set off, down the steep narrow road into Stroud and up the far side, heading south-westwards, towards the Bath road. It was noon when I reached Chipping Sodbury and dawdled up the wide, sunny street. Coming to the top, where the little town ends, I stopped beside the " Grapes " and watched the potman leisurely open the door—to show that the hour had arrived when a traveller could lawfully assuage his thirst.

The bar was empty and I went in and sat down but soon customers began to drift in and I listened to the broad Gloucestershire voices talking of the week's happenings. Presently the conversation turned to the coming " Mop " fair.

So I joined in and asked if a cheese fair was ever held in the town. After the silence that always greets a stranger, my question was answered by a chorus of " No." " But I thought Chipping Sodbury was famous for cheese," I queried, rather mendaciously. Again I was wrong but, not to be defeated, I asked, " Are there any farms around where they still make cheese ? "

" They used to make sum down't Mr. Martin's . . . That were in th' old man's time." Then after a pause. " They ain't made no cheese there since I can remember." I waited for more. " I reckon you'll 'ave to go Stinchcombe way. Ask Bob Ruddick, 'e'll know. Ay, ask Bob."

Bob Ruddick, he knew because he worked as a lad on a farm where they made the cheeses and where, for all he knew, they still made 'em. He were pretty certain they did still make 'em and if it weren't Davis' Farm then it might be another, for up in the Berkeley Vale was the cheese-making country and if you went up along the Gloucester Road or along under Stinchcombe, you'd be sure to find ones that still made 'em. Though (mind you) there ain't many of 'em left now . . . and so, I finished my pint and made for Berkeley.

The scent was hot there and my spirits rose when the barmaid of the " Berkeley Arms " told me of Mrs. Browning's, not four miles off—and it was there at Actree's Farm—a stone's throw from the Bristol-Gloucester road that I found cheese, and peace.

The farm—brick, snug, set down fairly and spaciously among its out-buildings—was a fitting place and Mrs. Browning (like Elizabeth Barrett) a poetess, only of cheeses.

She took me to the dairy and showed me all the implements of her art. The big iron presses and vats and the round wooden troughs—all so ancient and so English and for which few modern substitutes have been found—and then, in turn, into the great garret under the roof beams where stood all the cheeses—great and small, double and single, baby cheeses and giant cheeses—slowly ripening. All earmarked for special customers—many for London clubs—such is Mrs. Browning's fame.

Then I was told how carefully the cows have to be watched and herded. Should they stray on to a wrong pasture then the cheese is spoiled. Neither must there be too much richness in the milk. The butter-producing cow cannot give cheese milk, mark you.

And then all the questions of temperatures and cultures. No wonder that the weeks of cheese-making mean constant anxiety and little sleep. So I was taken to the kitchen and shown the red and blue cards, many framed on the walls, of prizes gained and, best of all, I was given a taste of Prime Double Gloucester.

What more could man wish for?

IV.
CHEDDAR

IV.—CHEDDAR

By Horace Annesley Vachell

For the everyday, cut-and-come-again cheese I commend with all my heart the Cheddar. Other cheeses have their seasons; the Cheddar, as an adjunct to luncheon and dinner, as a neverfailing good companion to a glass (or two) of vintage port, is seasonable—as the good Mrs. Beeton puts it—all the year round. Living as I do in the West Country, not far from the Cheddar Gorge, I have to confess regretfully that the Cheddar cheese of commerce seldom comes from Cheddar. There is a story—probably apocryphal—of a lorry skidding and upsetting upon one of the green hills of Somerset. Cheddar cheeses made elsewhere rolled into Cheddar. Trippers visiting the Gorge carry away with them miniature cheeses born and bred in Canada. In fact, although it is held to be foolish to carry coals to Newcastle, cheeses are carried to Cheddar!

Nevertheless Cheddar, deliciously creamy, with nothing " soapy " about it, is still made near Cheddar, a village at the foot of the Gorge, perilously overhung by the limestone cliffs. Huge boulders roll down into the gorge, but not one, so far as I know, has crashed into a cheese. Here, too, are the caves.

Cheeses are divided for trade purposes into two classes, hard and soft. Cheddar is hard, the typically pressed cheese, and the most important of its kind produced in this country. Stilton is an unpressed hard cheese, ripened by the aid of the blue mould which grows in veins within it. The best

Cheddar is made from whole milk, like Cheshire. Canadian Cheddar does not greatly differ from English or Scotch Cheddar, but it may be manufactured from partially skimmed milk. So far as I can learn, the Cheddar cheese made in the valleys near Cheddar, in Wiltshire and Dorset is never made from partially skimmed milk.

Last October I assisted (in the Pump Room at Bath) at a Cheddar cheese competition, and I carried away with me a fine chunk of the prize-winning cheese of a firm and wax-like consistency, delicately flavoured, about as good as it could be. Why Cheddar varies so much in quality and flavour is easily explained. The best cheese—no matter where it comes from —is made at the right time of year when the pastures on which the cows graze are at their best and richest. Cheese made from milk when the cows are fed on fodder is inferior. One can amplify this crude statement. Certain pastures are so rich in certain grasses that the farmers (although methods are identical) who own these favoured meadows make more delicately flavoured cheeses than their next-door neighbours. A viticulturist can take cuttings from the Cabernet-Sauvignon grape, plant those cuttings on soil similar to the soil of a famous vineyard, employ a wine-maker from that vineyard, and—despite skill and care—is unable to make a wine comparable with any of the " first growths." In the course of centuries something has been taken from and added to the soil of, let us say, the Château Lafite Vineyard by the vine itself. A famous vineyard, in a very true sense, makes itself.

Be that as it may, Cheddar cheese varies disconcertingly. Stewards of famous clubs acquire great *expertise* in selecting cheeses ; and any young member, who aspires to be a gourmet, is well advised to ask the Great Panjandrum of the Coffee Room what cheese is in season. Brazil nuts are an excellent

"VARIETY IS A GOOD THING"

adjunct to port, but they are only fit to eat when they come fresh from Brazil, free from any taint of rancidity.

Fortunately, thanks to the different sizes of Cheddar, and the time it takes to ripen, it is possible to enjoy this particular cheese all the year round. Unfortunately, however, the ordinary Man in the Street is at the mercy of the tradesman who sells the cheese. I asked a salesman, who invariably is kind enough to consider my palate, if customers (taking them by and large) knew the difference between good, bad and indifferent Cheddar. He assured me, with a twinkle in his eye, that they did not.

With milk retailed at threepence a pint, it is amazing that cheese can be made and sold at a reasonable profit. Happily, I am not concerned with certain trade mysteries. If, as I am informed, it does not pay to make butter and cheese in England provided you can market your milk, how is it that Canadian Cheddar can be sold at elevenpence a pound and New Zealand butter at 1s. 6d. a pound, when Canada is three

"ASKS FOR A POUND OF CHEDDAR . . . AS . . . FOR A POUND OF FLOUR."

thousand miles away from the English market and New Zealand fourteen thousand miles?

A housewife asks for a pound of Cheddar as she asks for a pound of flour, takes it home, sets it before the family who eat it with humble, we may presume, rather than grateful hearts. It is, however, a solacing thought that indifferent Cheddar, although the better quality is preferable, makes " a dish of cheese " fit for the gods. The recipe of this I published in my *This Was England* and I seize the opportunity of setting down here that I received letters from all parts of the Empire thanking me for printing it. This recipe was cherished by an aunt of mine. On one occasion a great personage was dining with her; and she gave him this dish of cheese. He asked for the recipe. My aunt asked an important question: " Is this, Sir, a royal command? " Her guest replied, " No, no, I ask as your guest." My aunt laughed. " I refuse," said she, " to give this recipe to guests, because I hope they will come again to eat it at my table." This particular guest assured her that he would come again—and he did. The recipe was given to me, grudgingly, on the condition that I did not publish it in my aunt's lifetime. But, before I was at liberty to play the part of a public benefactor, a lady of my acquaintance begged me to break my solemn pledge on the altar of friendship. When I refused, she coaxed me to come to her house to make this dish for her guests. The ingredients, *plus* a chafing-dish, would be placed—so she assured me—behind a tall screen in the dining-room. And here, secure from any Peeping Tom, I could play the part of the Regent of France, Philippe d'Orleans, who delighted to cook special *plats* for his guests. I promised to do this, but, familiar with the guiles and wiles of the Fair, I bespoke not only the necessary ingredients but two others. I found everything laid out; I made the dish; and it was acclaimed with enthusiasm as the " best ever." A week later, I met this lady. She shook her fist at me. " You devil! " Her husband told me that three times had his wife essayed to make the dish, before she guessed that I had been taking gross liberties with her underpinning. Here is the recipe:

Cut half a pound of Cheddar cheese into thin slices and put them in a stew pan. Add three tablespoonfuls of milk and a gill of cream, the yolks of three eggs and the whites of two. Season with pepper and salt.

Whip it until it boils—and it is done.

Let your guests be handed squares of toast. Let the cheese be served in a dish. The guests will spread the hot cheese on the hot toast. The boiling cheese should be free from lumps, smooth as mayonnaise sauce and about the same consistency.

Unlike Welsh rarebit, this dish of cheese is easily digested.

I can find no mention of Cheddar cheese in my *Dictionary of Quotations*. Shakespeare mentions Banbury cheese. Bardolph calls Slender a Banbury cheese in allusion to the thin carcase of Slender. Nobody could indict the best Cheddar as being thin; it is agreeably full-bodied, plump as a well-nourished dairymaid. Bad Cheddar is soapy, villainously so. The noble cheese that was accorded first prize in our Pump Room had the texture of the best Gruyère. A kinsman of mine, now in his eightieth year, eats Cheddar cheese after luncheon and dinner nearly every day of the year. I have not asked him whether he attributes his robust health to this constant absorption of Cheddar or to the glass of vintage port which he sips with it. Heavenly twins they are! God's Good Creatures.

Hone, in one of his fat, informative books, mentions a gentleman whose mother dreamed before he was born that he would become an ostrich. His birth took place in a rocky cave near the Peak of Derbyshire. As a child he could make a hearty breakfast off pebbles. When other boys ate cherry pie, he was content to be apportioned the stones. Later on, he served oysters to his guests and ate the shells. Marbles were a *bonne bouche*. Bigger boys used to pick him up and shake him to hear the marbles rattling in his stomach. But, to his dying day, he swore solemnly that he could not digest —*cheese*.

Is it true that cheese can digest everything except itself?

Lean, in his delightful *Collectanea,* cites a proverb which confirms the affirmation that too rich milk does not make the best Cheddar cheese. "The more butter, the worse cheese." The gammers in Somerset used to say: "Bad cheese asks butter to eat with it; good cheese asks none." The same gossips, not so very long ago, were insistent that the first cut of a Cheddar cheese should be divided amongst the maids living in any house where a child was born. This secured fecundity to them when they married.

Does cheese breed melancholy? Old Burton may have something to say about that. Fuller, in his *Worthies,* confesses that he can't understand why some people have an antipathy to cheese. Nor can I. But, for my part, I can't understand why some gentlemen prefer blondes to brunettes.

Camden, in his *Britannia,* affirms that the Romans taught the Britons how to make cheese. Writing in 1586, he goes on to say: "West of Wells, just under the Mendippe Hills, lies Cheddar, famous for its excellent and prodigious cheeses made there, some of which require more than a man's strength to put them on the table, and of a delicate taste, equalling if not excelling that of Parmesan."

In 1635 Lord Conway wrote to Lord Poulet to remind him of the cheese of Cheddar which had been promised to him. Lord Poulet, answering this letter, observed that Cheddar cheeses were held in such esteem at Court and by the nobility that they "are long bespoken before they are made."

In 1638 Sir Philip Percivalle, an Irish statesman, prayed his cousin to "bestow what surplus there may be from rents in the purchase of an old cheese called Cheddar."

We come now to John Locke, the Somerset philosopher, whose talk was "such a happy union of wit and good sense." Did Locke make cheese? He received a letter from the Earl of Salisbury: "You have recovered your skill in

51

"A MONSTROUS CHEESE MADE FOR LORD WEYMOUTH ... WAS BIG ENOUGH TO HOLD A GIRL OF THIRTEEN."

Cheddar cheese and have sent me one of the best ever seen."

Daniel Defoe, in his *Tour,* published in 1725, writes : " The whole village of Cheddar are cow-keepers," and he speaks of a monstrous cheese made for Lord Weymouth which, when scooped out, was big enough to hold a girl of thirteen!

Probably the biggest Cheddar cheese ever made, weighing eleven hundredweight, measuring in circumference nine feet, four inches and twenty inches in depth, was presented to Queen Victoria.

In 1856 the Joseph Harding system of making Cheddar was reckoned to be the best, till another system superseded it, made public by Mr. Theodore Candy. Archdeacon Denison proclaimed far and wide the virtues of Cheddar cheese and kept one cheese for forty years!

In 1851 the best Cheddar fetched seventy shillings the hundredweight ; fifty years later, in 1900, similar cheese was sold in Bath at sixty-eight shillings the hundredweight, an amazing uniformity of price.

Other cheeses may vary in the making, but the manufacture of Cheddar was developed by Somerset farmers on precise and scientific *formulae*. I am writing these lines after a visit to a farm, where the " best " Cheddar is made. I was delightfully welcomed by the cheesemaker, who " put me wise " to the up-to-date methods. According to this expert (her cheeses win prizes) the cows on this farm are Shorthorns. Jersey cows produce too rich milk, Frisian-Holsteins give milk not quite rich enough. On this farm cheese is made all the year round, but the best cheese, please mark you, is vatted during the six months after April 1st, when the cows feed on the meadow grasses and clover ; and, again, of these six months, May and June have pride of place. The other six months, when cows are fed on fodder, do not lend themselves to the making of

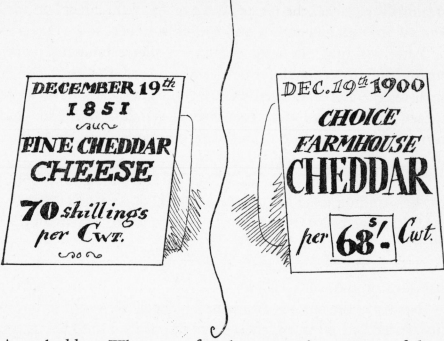

A.1. cheddar. When—as often happens—the cows are fed on turnips—the cheese is paler in colour, and has a peculiar taste. Hay, cake and kale are the usual fodder.

So far as I can ascertain, there is no farm making cheeses within four miles of Cheddar.

This is the procedure :

The morning and evening milkings are poured into an exquisitely clean vat which holds enough milk, about 400 gallons, to make *one* 76-lb cheese. The different milkings secure the right acidity : 2.1 or 2.2 on the acidemeter. The temperature should be 85° Fahrenheit.

Rennet (of any well-known brand) is added, one drachm to four gallons. After some five and twenty minutes the curd formed is " broken " (1) by vertical American Curd Knives and (2) by horizontal Curd Knives. This takes about fifteen minutes.

Then the curd, now in very small pieces, is scalded with steam till it reaches the temperature of 98° Fahrenheit, or 100° Far., if the summer is hot and the milk richer.

After scalding, the curd is cut into slices about ten inches square and three inches thick, and laid on the curd cooler with cheese cloth between each layer. The layers have to be turned ten minutes after they are placed in the cooler, and turned again and again every twenty minutes until the acidity of 7.5 to 8 is registered by the meter.

These layers are then placed for fifteen minutes (or more) in the grinding machine till the curd has cooled to 75° Far.

Salt is well worked in, about three ounces to a pound of curd.

The curd is then vatted, and the cheese is subjected to a pressure of about fifteen cwt.

Next day the cheeses are turned. The cloth is wrung out in hot water and replaced, the cheese is put back into the press, and the pressure is increased to twenty cwt.

Upon the second day, the cloth is again removed, the cheese is thinly coated with lard, and fresh cloth—" caps " for top and bottom, " side-pieces " to encircle—is put on. It is re-pressed.

On the third day, the cheese is bandaged with thicker cloth and transferred to the ripening room, where it is again turned each day for one week and afterwards twice a week. It will be ready to eat in about three months.

I saw about 200 cheeses averaging 76 lbs. a piece in the ripening loft. A small cheese called a Truckle weighs from seven to ten pounds and ripens much more quickly.

No colouring matter is used in this dairy.

What I did not know, what is worth knowing to any housekeeper, is that a Cheddar cheese made in June and ready for market in September can be bought and will keep for many months, cutting from it what is required. The connoisseur, therefore, is well advised to buy Cheddar cheese when it is at its best in September or October, and to make sure that it comes from Wiltshire, Dorset or Somerset, from a prize-winning farmer. Don't buy Cheddar cheese made during the six months when the cows are fed on fodder.

The ordinary Welsh Rarebit does not exact the best Cheddar.

It is, on the contrary, better, and more easily made, from the coloured Cheddars manufactured in Canada and New Zealand.

Cheddar cheese varies in price from eleven to eighteen pence a pound.

In Bath the sale of Cheddar cheese is greater than the sale of all other cheeses, including foreign cheeses. Whether this can be said in Edinburgh or Dublin I do not know. It is—so a salesman informs me—a lamentable fact that in Somerset, the cradle of this cheese, not one housewife out of ten knows the difference between the genuine article and its counterfeit presentment. I asked one lady of the larder how she kept Cheddar cheese. Her eyes twinkled.

" We don't keep cheese ; we eats it."

" But if some friend presented you with a 76-lb. cheese, what would you do with it ? "

" We'd just have to give away what we couldn't eat ourselves."

However, another more thrifty housewife assured an ignoramus who too often wants to know more than he can find out that a big Cheddar cheese can be kept for two years in excellent condition if placed in a cool room, turned over every other day and carefully wiped with a dry cloth. If any philanthropist, who reads this paragraph, is generous enough to send me a huge Cheddar cheese, I pledge myself to try this experiment and report results.

The farm which I have just visited charmed my eye before I entered the dairy. I saw with satisfaction buildings of time-mellowed brick, lush pastures free from weeds, a pellucid stream meandering through the meadows, well-trimmed fences, and a herd of handsome cows. There were the outward and visible signs of a prosperous industry. Within, I repeat, the scrupulous cleanliness of the dairy (and everything in it) was richly reassuring. I wished to visit the dairy in Dorset which secured the First Prize for Cheddar in the Bath Competition, but it is relevant to mention that on this particular farm no cheese is made before the 1st May.

I shall conclude with a story concerning an immense Cheddar cheese, made for an enterprising gentleman who might be called a sometime uncrowned Monarch of Grocers.

This gargantuan cheese sustained a grievous fall and split

H

in two ! Into each half, the owner, fully alive to the hidden virtues of advertisement, stuffed many gold sovereigns. The cheese was exhibited in his shop window with this device : " Any customer buying a pound of this cheese may find a sovereign in it."

Unhappily, this was an infringement of the Lottery Act, and the grocer was so informed. Being a man of resource, he substituted another device : " Many sovereigns have been taken from this cheese in obedience to the Law, but, be careful, a tooth might be easily broken on a bit of gold ! "

He sold every pound at the top price.

Ave et Vale!

Vale, as a monosyllable, is indeed the first and last word where the making of the right Cheddar cheese is concerned. The rich vales of Dorset, Wilts and Somerset are much as they were when Milton wrote *L'Allegro*.

Meadows trim with daisies pied . . .

Surely the savoury dish shared by Corydon and Thyrsis was Cheddar cheese with its lubricant—the spicy nut-brown ale. A country " mess " in a west country setting. I like to think of Corydon as a simple brewer of good stingo, of Thyrsis as a champion cheese-maker. Euphrosyne must have bestowed her graces and benedictions on the comely pair. In the same spirit, I bestow my valedictory blessing on all who are already abundantly blessed when they eat the best Cheddar cheese.

V.
CHESHIRE

V.—CHESHIRE CHEESE

By Vyvyan Holland

Dans le Chester sec et rose
A longues dents, l'Anglais mord.

Victor Meusy.

"Very little," observed Mr. Oldmeadow, when I plucked up courage to ask him to tell me something about Cheshire cheese, "can be said about any kind of cheese, beyond a description of the technical details of its manufacture. The only way to learn about cheese is to eat it."

The principle contained in this observation is largely true as applied to all criticism except, possibly, literary criticism. The only way to understand music is to listen to it ; the only way to appreciate painting is to look at it ; literature, however, can be criticised in words because words are the medium of expression employed in the matter to be criticised.

The only other person I asked, a native of Cheshire, replied : "Cheese ? Oh! Yes. You eat it with biscuits and it smells." Not very constructive either.

So, although to write at any great length upon Cheshire cheese might have been child's play for the late Monsieur Marivaux, it has presented a nice problem to me. The problem is further complicated by the fact that whatever I say will probably be read by people who make a profession of cheese, so that it cannot be solved by just giving rein to my imagination, which would merely result in my being set upon by hordes of indignant turophiles.

It is significant of the difficulty which attends the subject of cheese that even Casanova found the task of writing about it beyond him. He says (Vol. VI., Chap. III.) : "I had undertaken to write a dictionary of cheese, but I had to abandon the work, having recognised that the undertaking was beyond my powers, in the same way that J. J. Rousseau found the subject of botany to be beyond his." Mr. T. W. Earp, probably the most eminent Casanova scholar of these isles, tells me that this is the only occasion upon which Casanova ever admitted that there was anything at all that he could not do. So how should I, who am clearly no Casanova, succeed in doing something which he dared not even attempt ?

Cheshire cheese is a hard cheese, made from cows' milk, like Cheddar. But, unlike Cheddar, it cannot be imitated anywhere in the world, and one can be perfectly certain, when confronted with a Cheshire cheese, that it was actually made in the county of Cheshire. The reason that it cannot be imitated is that it derives its peculiar qualities from the fact that the soil of Cheshire contains rich deposits of salt, which impart a very high degree of salinity to the milk of most Cheshire-grazed cattle. It is probably this salinity which gives Cheshire cheese its strongest characteristic, namely that of slow ripening.

Camden described the county of Cheshire as being " tritici et farris jejuna," and, according to Mr. George Ormerod, in his monumental *History of Cheshire*, until late in the nineteenth century it was considered that Cheshire farmers raised only what was sufficient for their own consumption and paid their rent by cheese. Mr. Ormerod says that the cheese which was most esteemed in those days was made on farms on which " the powers of subterranean salt springs are supposed to operate favourably," particularly in the vicinity of Nantwich and Middlewich. It is recorded that three hundred tons of Cheshire cheese were ordered for the troops in Scotland during the Civil War. In fact, salt and cheese have been the chief industries in Cheshire from time immemorial, and the natives of Cheshire are more proud of their cheese than of any other of their products.

Cheshire cheese is of three varieties, namely, as one might expect from a true British cheese, red, white and blue. The most usual form is the red. The red colour is obtained by the use of a vegetable dye called annatto, which comes from South America and the West Indies; the best cheese is coloured in this way, and it is usually this cheese which, when allowed to mature, becomes the Old Blue Cheshire which is so sought after and so comparatively rarely encountered. White Cheshire, which is really pale yellow, is also slightly dyed; its manufacture differs in a few slight points from that of the red cheese, with the result that it matures very much more quickly and is therefore more commercially profitable, as it can be sold so much sooner. However, all Blue Cheshire does not start as Red Cheshire, and Mr. A. J. A. Symons mentions a memorable Blue Cheshire he enjoyed at Scotts (Wine and Food, Vol. XIV., p. 63) which he describes as being "not the usual crumbly Blue Cheshire, but a wonder of rich, creamy softness : an undying gastronomic memory." Even allowing for the natural enthusiasm of the gastronome, this has a very soothing sound, and it was no doubt a cheese of this sort, discovered in and filched from the larder of the Queen of Hearts, that accounted for the contented grin on the face of the Cheshire Cat in *Alice in Wonderland*.

There are also three methods of manufacturing Cheshire cheese and each method produces a special type, differing from

"THE BEST JUDGES OF GOOD CHEESE."

the others by the length of time that it takes to ripen. These methods are known as the early-ripening, the medium-ripening and the long-keeping, the last two producing a much higher quality cheese than the first. The early-ripening cheese is only made until the end of April or the middle of May, or so long as there is a heavy demand for cheese for immediate consumption, as if kept for any length of time it would develop too much acidity and become bitter. The medium-ripening cheese is made in May, June and September and is ready for sale about six weeks after manufacture. The long-keeping cheese is made

64

August, and it is this that develops in time into

ire. An old Blue Cheshire is usually from four to

ths old, though sometimes the cheeses are kept as

teen months and I know of at least one case where

s supposed to have been three years old. And,

subject of the age of Cheshire cheese, I remember a

by my friend Mr. T. C. Dugdale, R.A., who was

ashire. He told me that one Mr. Lavery, a famous

in the Old Market Place in Manchester, always

hire cheese at which the mice had been, " as they

judges of a good cheese." And yet I am told that

is sometimes unsaleable in Lancashire and has to

more discerning South for disposal. Sir Francis

myss, out of whom I tried to get some useful

r this chapter, tells me that before the War

a cheese manufacturer in Gloucestershire dis-

paring to destroy a large, beautifully ripe Blue

ng unsaleable. He assures me that the destruc-

ke place!

rocess of manufacture is very much akin to

and its success largely depends upon the care

temperature is kept regulated throughout the

It is of no particular interest except to the

urer. A very clear, short description of the

ibed in *Cheese and Cheese-making* by James

at is highly technical. It should be mentioned,

e more rennet that is used, the more lactic

in the curd and this causes more rapid ripening.

keeping cheese, lactic acid is not intentionally
developed at all. The main difference between the process of
manufacture of Cheshire cheese and of soft cheeses like Stilton
or Wensleydale is that during the manufacture of Cheshire

cheese it is subjected to very considerable pressure to expel the whey. The distinguishing characteristics of the finished cheese are its sharp, salty taste and its firm texture (produced by the pressure) which is neither flaky nor waxy, but a compromise between the two.

The size of the finished cheese varies very considerably and it may be anything from ten to a hundred lbs in weight. In 1825 the inhabitants of the Palatine of Chester presented H.R.H. the Duke of York with a cheese weighing 149 lbs. This was, at the time said to be the largest Cheshire cheese ever made. Eighty-three years later, in 1908, one of the cheese that won the Gold Medal and Challenge Cup of the Cheshire cheese industry was presented to the King, who graciously accepted it. This cheese weighed 200 lbs. But this was eclipsed in 1909 when one Mr. Percy Cooke of Tattenhall Farm, near Chester, executed an order for twenty cheeses to weigh 300 lbs each, their total weight being over two and a half tons ! It is on record that the manufacture was a complete success and that the cheese was of excellent quality and flavour.

Cheshire cheese is the oldest English cheese. Or, rather, it is the oldest English cheese to which any reference can be found. According to the *Encyclopædia Britannica*, twelfth century writers refer to the excellence of Cheshire cheese ; but as no names are mentioned it is a little difficult to substantiate this. John Speed, the historian (1542-1629), referring to the produce of the country of Cheshire, says : " The champion grounds make glad the hearts of their tillers ; the meadows imborded with divers sweet-smelling flowers ; and the pastures makes the kines udders to strout to the paile, from whom and wherein the best cheese in all Europe is made."

And Sir Kenelme Digby, in the seventeenth century, in his *Closet open'd*," refers to Cheshire cheese as a " quick,

PRESENTED H.R.H WITH A CHEESE WEIGHING 149 LBS.

fat, rich, well-tasted cheese to serve melted upon a piece of toast."

Indeed, the very high cream-content of Cheshire cheese makes it pre-eminently suitable for the making of toasted cheese, as more than one tavern in Fleet Street will tell you : and it is to be observed that it is the red cheese which is used for this purpose, not the white, which is not so rich and succulent. Apart from the making of toasted cheese, Cheshire cheese is not as a rule very suitable for the making of cheese dishes or savouries, though a most pleasant savoury can be produced by mixing equal quantities of grated Cheshire and Parmesan cheese with a little cream, seasoning them with salt and pepper and inserting the mixture between two un-sweetened wafers, afterwards baking it in a hot oven for about seven minutes. I am indebted to Mr. Ambrose Heath's excellent little book, *Good Savouries*, for this recipe.

At any rate, Cheshire cheese was famous abroad long before Stilton or any other English cheese. This probably accounts for the fact that in any mention of English cheese " Chester " always finds a prominent place. *The Encyclopedia Universál Ilustrada Europeo-Americano*, probably the most compre-hesive Encyclopædia in the world, published over a period of 30 years in Barcelona and consisting, with Appendices, of eighty volumes, mentions only Chester, Dunlop, Gloucester and Norfolk as English cheeses ! And yet this is strange because the fragile and brittle nature of Cheshire cheese renders it unsuitable for exportation purposes.

Maurice des Ombiaux, in his excellent little book *Les Fromages*, observes : " How much more delectable is ale when one takes care to give it a good piece of ' Chester ' for a companion." He puts it higher than Stilton, although declaring that the English prefer Stilton. For a Frenchman to mention any foreign alimentary preparation at all is already a very high honour. From Maurice des Ombiaux also comes the suggestion that some people replace celery in eating 'Chester' with celery salt and he suggests that celery salt should be kept for the many meat extracts which disfigure the shelves of the English grocer's shop. He concludes his remarks about 'Chester' by saying : "There is nothing anæmic about it as in other cheeses. It is, on the contrary, high in colour as a Scotsman fresh from his mountains, for whom whisky has no terrors."

Cheshire cheese is no food for weaklings and is, it may be observed, discouraged by many dietitians, particularly when consumed, as Providence meant it to be, with bread. Bread and cheese, we are told, belong to different groups of vitamins or starches or sugars or some such thing, and are vitally indigestible when taken together. But let us not heed such warnings, which are but the peevish vapourings of the jealous dyspeptic and, as such, do not apply to you or to me.

No chapter on Cheshire cheese is complete without a reference to the "Rich Crops Twice a Day" Legend. I have come across several versions of this, and quote three of them to show how a legend can vary. In Stephens *Book of the Farm* it is given as follows :—

A West Indian planter, some generations ago, was boasting in a Cheshire dairy farmer's house of the fruits they grew in Jamaica, two crops in one year. The farmer fetched a huge Cheshire cheese. "This he said, is the fruit we grow here once, or even twice a day."

Legends of the Dee by C. H. Longrigg supplies us with the following :—

69

CHESHIRE CHEESE

A legend of the Cheese Stage, Cheshire

The " Pride of the Dee " at the Cheese stage lay moored,
With her cargo of cheese in the hold safe secured ;
And her captain, Jack Chester, sat chatting away
With Fernandez, a Spaniard vivacious and gay,
Whose brigantine anchored in midstream close by
Was the joy of his heart and the pride of his eye.
Now we talk of a ship as a " tight little craft,"
And sailors the " tightest of lads that e'er laughed,"
If grog they have had or had not, which may be
A natural outcome of " being at sea ; "
And Fernandez and Chester were tight, it is true
In this nautical sense, and began to review
The merits of England and Spain, when Jack said
His land was the better ; Fernandez flushed red,
And banging his fist on the table replied,
The truth of that statement he flatly denied,
And added some lighter expressions beside—
" My land," quoth the Spaniard, " bears crops twice a year,
Rich produce and fruits and wine that will cheer
The heart of a man. There is no such in thine."
Jack Chester stepped out and soon brought in a fine
Large Cheshire cheese, and said he, " Now look you here !
Your country produces rich crops twice a year !
Of this that I bring in my hands I may say
My country produces rich crops twice a day ! "

And finally, Mr. Osbert Burdett, in his " *Little Book of Cheese*," quotes the following first and second verses of :

70

"FERNANDEZ, A SPANIARD VIVACIOUS AND GAY."

A Cheshireman sailed into Spain
  To trade for merchandize ;
When he arrived from the main
  A Spaniard him espies.
Who said, You English rogue, look here !
  What fruits and spices fine
Our land produces twice a year.
  Thou hast not such in thine.

The Cheshireman ran to his hold
  And fetched a Cheshire cheese,
And said, Look here, you dog, behold !
  We have such fruits as these.
Your fruits are ripe but twice a year,
  As you yourself do say,
But such as I present you here
  Our land brings twice a day.

To many people, particularly to visitors to England from abroad, the words " Cheshire Cheese " are mainly connected with the hostelry in Fleet Street bearing that name. Although " The Old Cheshire Cheese " is most universally known for the steak, kidney and oyster pudding which is served there in the autumn and winter months, it is also justly proud of its cheese. Nowhere can one get a more delicious dish of toasted cheese made, as I have observed earlier, from the Red Cheshire : the White Cheshire is never cooked there, but is served with radishes or watercress or celery when in season. And it is pleasant to sit there in the chair that tradition declares to have been used by Dr. Samuel Johnson, among surroundings which have not changed since his day. Here, also, at the end of the nineteenth century, the Rhymers' Club used to hold its meetings. This club was a gathering of young authors and artists of the nineties, and included among its members Max Beerbohm, Bernard Shaw, Ernest Dowson, Charles Conder, W. B. Yeats, Joseph Conrad and Aubrey Beardsley. A long account of the activities of this club is given by Mr. W. B. Yeats in his autobiographical work, *The Trembling of the Veil,* which is one of the most interesting books of its kind ever written.

And that is all that I can say about Cheshire cheese, except one thing, which is, in a way, the most important of all. And that is that for a family whose consumption of cheese is small there is no cheese like Cheshire, because it is the only cheese that, if the right kind be bought, will last for weeks without showing any sign of deterioration and without constantly thrusting its presence upon one's notice by its aroma.

VI.
DOUBLE   GLOUCESTER

VI.—DOUBLE GLOUCESTER

By Osbert Burdett

It is no surprise that a cheese should vary in shape and colour, for these are matters of taste ; and different tastes create different markets. But it is odd that Double Gloucester should be known in two forms and colours and that those familiar with one, as several correspondents assure me, have never seen the other. This difference is quite separate from the recognised difference between Single and Double Gloucester cheese.

In London, we know the latter as a red cheese the shape of a millstone, and we esteem it the aristocrat of English red cheeses. It is pregnant but subtle in flavour, and surpasses in delicacy good red Cheshire itself. One can pass from Cheshire to Double Gloucester as from a fine bourgeois to a fine vintage wine. From the point of view of a consumer, its season is short, for it arrives on the market with autumn and is usually not to be had in London after Christmas. Double Gloucester is perhaps the single hard English cheese that can be compared for richness and delicacy of flavour with the great blue cheeses.

Locally, however, it is known mainly as a white or yellow cheese, and those the writer saw at a display of West Country cheeses last autumn were also of the round loaf-shape familiar in Cheddar. Inquiries from local makers leave it uncertain whence the London market is supplied. One Gloucester buyer suggested that the red Double Gloucesters were made in Dairy Schools for London cheesemongers.

In the following remarks, then, the cheese discussed and praised is that supplied for the London market, since the comparisons I have been able to make between this and that obtained direct from makers in the county shows sad differences in texture, quality and flavour. To repeat: the Double Gloucesters we prize in London are red, millstone in shape, hard, close in texture, and exquisitely flavoured—pungent without being sharp, and so mellow that the tiniest morsel is pregnant : in a word like a glorified Cheshire cheese. That I have tasted in Bath or received from the county is yellow, in shape either a loaf or a millstone, soft in texture, very mild, and, to speak frankly, of poorest quality.

Of course neither the colour nor the shape explains this difference ; but, since it is convenient to be able to recognise a fine cheese at sight, it is only fair to the reader to add that the shape and colour familiar in London should be borne in mind. They have never proved a disappointment.

The real difference, no doubt, is that the London cheeses have been carefully chosen and fully matured, whereas those obtained from the county have been far too young, unmatured, and consequently lacking in quality. The difference in price indicates this. Double Cloucester in London can never be had for less than eighteen pence a pound. Those from the county cost only ten pence. Again, matured cheeses are nowadays appreciated by few ; and it may, alas, well be true that there is next to no local demand for them ; whereas in London, the chief demand coming from men's clubs where a great cheese is expected and keenly appreciated, the only Double Gloucesters wanted are the fully matured and superbly flavoured. To attain this quality the cheesemongers have to wait and keep their cheeses long in store, which of course is an extra expense to them. From the superior hardness of the London variety we can judge their age which may well be a year, whereas a cheese ready for marketing will be no more than six months. These remarks are no attack on the county cheese-makers ; but on their local customers. They do imply, however, that local taste is less discriminating than that of London clubs ; and therefore that it is nowadays the London taste alone that maintains the fine quality of the original and rightly famous Double Gloucester.

From the county I have had specimens not only soft in texture but with many seams and fissures—in deplorable contrast to the close and crumbly texture of the true, matured cheese. A Dairy Instructor also informs me that Cheddar makers have unfortunately of late taken to making a soft type of Cheddar, selling this as Gloucester, and even taking prizes with it at Dairy Shows. One is constantly hearing of the little faith now placed in the judges and verdicts of these Shows. The moral is that consumers alone are the guardians of quality. Hence the hope of such books as this to stimulate knowledge and interest outside their last stronghold, the London clubs.

The name Double refers to the size, though the methods of making the two distinct cheeses are not very dissimilar. Single Gloucester is a quick-ripening cheese. Double needs six months before it is ready for the market, and then those cheesemen who cater for discriminating customers will still store it until its full maturity shall have been reached. In all hard cheeses size is essential for quality. Only the big cheeses will mature properly. The reader should be warned against all diminutive cheeses bearing famous names because they are mockeries of the true cheese. Double Gloucester keeps well; and these fine, old cheeses used to be sent down the Thames from Lechlade on barges that they might be enjoyed with vintage port. In those days, wrote a local reviewer who thought the mention of red Double Gloucesters in *A Little Book of Cheese* to be a slip, " they were stained dark red—on the outside—with the edges rubbed to show a natural rich colour." How this "painting" came to be we shall see in a moment: the original (and present) colour of the rind is a dull blue on the sides of the millstone and orange-yellow on the rims.

References abound to show that Gloucester was prized in its mature state ; that it was a connoisseur's joy, and that its weight consequently would run from 50 lbs to 60 lbs.

Our trouble at the moment is that most people will not look at matured cheese because, interest having been lost in English foods, cheese has come to mean something neither local nor personal, something that can be bought without discrimination and eaten, not for its own sake, but as a mere adjunct to a meal. Few women are cheese-eaters. Few men will help them with the larder. The attitude of both has come to be that of Mr. Jorrocks who declined Mrs. Markham's offer of sweets with the remark : " No ; I'll fill up the chinks wi' cheese." Actually, the kinship between fine cheese and good wine is so close that neglect of one encourages neglect of the other. What irony that, though England is not a country of the vine, our men of letters have kept the great literature of wine in full vigour ; while the great cheeses that England still produces have inspired almost no literature in praise of them.

Double Gloucester is always mentioned by our agricultural writers as a famous cheese, but the date given for its first making is certainly too late. Professor Thorold Rogers, in his *History of Argiculture and Prices*, says that it was first made in 1772 ; but, since he gave the previous year for Stilton—which we know[1] to have been made early in the eighteenth century— we may be that Double certain Gloucester was well established

[1]From William Marshall's *Rural Economy*, see post.

at that date. It can scarcely have been a recent cheese that inspired Samuel Rudder to write thus of it, in 1779 :

" In this Vale (of Gloucester) is made that fine cheese so deservedly esteemed not only in Great Britain but in all countries wherever it has been carried. The hundreds of Berkeley, of Thornbury, and the lower division of Grumbald's Ash, produce the best.

" It is made of various thicknesses, from about ten pounds to a quarter of a hundredweight each. The thick sort is called Double Gloucestershire, and Double Berkeley, and usually sells upon the spot at sixpence a pound. It requires to be kept to an age proportionate to its size and thickness, to make it ready for the table." [1]

Again, the great authority for agriculture, cheese, and cider, William Marshall, who went to reside in Gloucestershire in 1783, mentions with special praise Mrs. Wade, the manager of the Maberley Dairy, Near Berkeley. "What renders her practice (he says) singularly valuable is that of its being the old-established practice, which brought the Berkeley cheese to its highest degree of excellency, unaltered, as that of most dairies has been, by modern deviations." [2] He speaks of her experience " during the last twenty or thirty years." [2] This would bring us to the late fifties at least. Indeed, cheese being older than all history, long famous cheeses like Double Gloucester could not have been perfected at a very late date.

In his preface William Marshall tells us that, before he made his home in the West of England, he had in Norfolk " made an essay in the art of manufacturing cheese, and I was desirous to become master of it." Since, in his other volumes—there were

[1] *A New History of Gloucestershire*—By Samuel Rudder. Cirencester, 1779.

[2] *The Rural Economy of Gloucestershire, including its Dairy* . . . *etc.*—By Mr. Marshall. 2 vols. 2nd edition, 1796. vol. 2, p. 106.

six in all, covering the Midland, the East Anglian, and some southern counties—we owe to him also the earliest details of Stilton, he is a writer to be grateful for. He is among the historians of English native foods and brews. " In the summer of 1783," he goes on, " I took up my residence in a farm house near the centre of the Vale of Gloucester : where, and in the Vale of Berkeley, I remained until I had exceeded my expectation with respect to the manufacturing of cheese."

Aiming at accuracy, most of his pages are devoted to minute descriptions of the methods of making and treating the curd in the two vales. In other words, they are primarily of interest to dairymen and to cheese-makers. These details, however, do not concern the eater of cheese more than the complexities of wine-making concern the wine drinker. We shall only touch on them, and can refer the curious first to the pages of Marshall himself and then to the shorter practical details given in Bulletin No. 43 on *Cheese-making*, issued by the Ministry of Agriculture.

For the general reader the interest of Marshall's pages is twofold. They are an invaluable record of early dairy practice; and, being written at a time when tradition and rule of thumb prevailed, they attempt, by comparing different methods favoured in different dairies, to secure such uniformity of right procedure as would help the dairy woman to be more " certain " of her results. Science, the introduction of the thermometer in place of " judging " was beginning to be invoked. Now, when the process of cheese-making has been reduced to a formula, and when dairy work has ceased to be a craft and become a trade, we in turn find the formula to be insufficient. Cheese-making, like wine-making, is a mystery so far as its finest products are concerned. The formula secures uniformity of the lower grades only. It is designed for factory practice ; but the

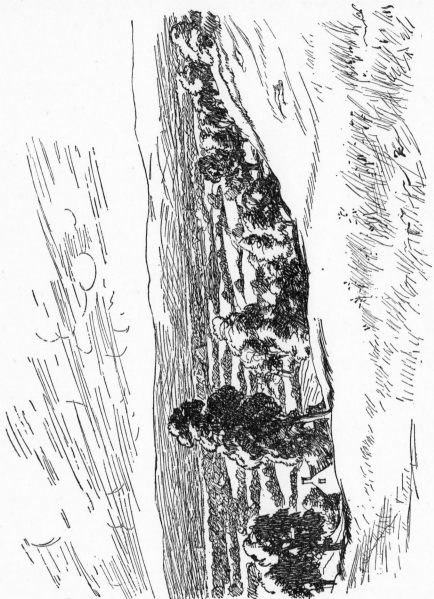

BERKELEY VALE—THE HOME OF GLOUCESTER CHEESE.

finer cheeses require in addition time, storage, and perhaps further nursing; luxuries that factories, intent on a quick turnover, are soullessly careless about. But in Marshall's day a man of his experience and observation was naturally anxious to reduce diverse and rule of thumb practices to better order.

Gloucestershire was a dairy country, and it was, he tells us, " the Gloucestershire breed of cows " which raised the local dairy to its greatest height. The chief product was not butter but cheese for which the country " has long been celebrated."

He speaks of two cheeses: " the best making " or made from fresh milk, preferably wholly unskimmed that it might have all its fat and richness; and " two meal cheese " made from a mixture. For this the evening's milk was set aside and skimmed the next morning when unskimmed new milk was added to it. The chief market, as we might expect, for " two meal cheese " was local. Being inferior, it was not known as Gloucester but sold at a lower price, under the name of Warwickshire cheese.

The cheese-making season was (and is) from the beginning of May until the end of October, and from Hone's *Table Book* we learn the honour once paid to cheese in Gloucestershire at the annual May Day celebrations:

" On the first of May, at the village of Randwick, near Stroud, there has been from time immemorial the following custom—Three large cheeses (Gloucester of course), decked with the gayest flowers of this lovely season, are placed on litters, equally adorned with flowers and boughs of trees waving at the corners. They are thus borne through the village accompanied by a joyous throng, shouting and huzzaaing with all their might and main, and usually accompanied by a little band of music. They proceed in this manner to the churchyard where the cheeses, being taken from the litters and

84

divested of their floral ornaments, are rolled three times round the church. They are then carried back in the same state, and in the midst of the village are cut up and distributed piecemeal to the inhabitants." [1]

Marshall does not mention this ancient custom. Confining himself strictly to dairy work, he describes each process in the two Vales of Gloucester and Berkeley. He particularly notices the " outer door opening into a small yard or garden " that distinguished the Gloucestershire dairy from the " cooped-up " room " with only a small window for air and light " deemed sufficient elsewhere. He then describes in turn the quality of the milk (used neat for the best cheese), the colouring, the making of rennet from " vells " or calves' stomachs, the coming of the curd that the rennet coagulates, and the breaking, gathering, scalding, vatting, pressing, salting, cleaning, storing and turning in the cheese-room, that complete the process.

It is interesting that Marshall thought the colouring of cheese (by annatto) to be " a crime," and he implies that the Gloucestershire dairywomen had invented the " deception." He says that they had " long practised it " and had probably heretofore " carried it on exclusively." As with butter, all of which is similarly coloured, the idea was to secure the richer yellow given naturally by some soils or in some seasons, because this tint gained a higher price. The example, therefore, spread to other counties. The Gloucestershire dairies also resorted to an interesting treatment of the rind.

In the cheese-room the floor was prepared " by rubbing it with bean tops, potato halm, or other green succulent herbage until it appears of a wet black colour." This was done with the intention of " encouraging the blue coat to rise." Here the

[1]Hone's *Table Book* (1878): see May Day Customs. This letter is signed C. Tomlinson and dated April, 1827.

cheeses were turned twice a week, and the floor prepared afresh once a fortnight. The rinds became " tough almost as leather " and were therefore well set for keeping.

In the Vale of Berkeley, only the " best making " cheese was made, but this in two thicknesses : the Single or thin and the thick or Double. The thin weighed from nine to twelve pounds, and the thick or Double up to twenty-five pounds. Describing the practices of the Berkeley dairies, he notes the same processes but again reverts to the colouring of the curd and had an additional section on " painting the rinds." Most of the thick cheese was made in this district, and was locally called not Double Gloucester but Double Berkeley. So much depended on the natural gifts of the dairy woman that " even the changing of a dairymaid has been observed to make a considerable difference." This is always true of every fine craft and must still be true despite the precison now possible by scientific methods. Even when the same assitants and cows were transported, it was found necessary to " know the ground" by two or three year's experience before good cheese could be made with certainty. He therefore held the management of a dairy to be even more important than the breed of cows.

The colouring used by the Berkeley dairies was supplied by the cheese factors (or merchants) who purchased their produce, so the charge of deception was admittedly dropped. To Marshall, however, it remained " an abominable practice." On the custom of " painting " the dairy women seemed to agree with him, for he says that they hated the labour of it.

It having been found that fine cheeses acquired by age a variegated surface which became " clouded with red," the practice was introduced of painting the rind. Marshall calls this " a late invention " and adds that all the dairy women disliked it. This painting gave a " characteristic " to Gloucestershire cheeses, and the factors soon found that they could not sell them as " Gloucesters " unless they possessed it. He implies that, once the practice of internal colouring had spread to other counties, it ceased to be a distinction, and therefore the painting of the rinds was resorted to. He foresaw that painting, too, would be imitated since " Gloucestershire is able to give the fashion to the colour of cheese." The native colour of the Gloucester rinds was " the superior blue of their sides and the golden hue of their edges." To this he hoped the County would revert, for he held that the natural colour " cannot be universally counterfeited." The painting was done in this way : After being cleaned, the rinds were treated with Spanish brown and Indian red, sometimes mixed and sometimes separately. The colour was either dabbed on wet with a cloth, or thrown dry in " pinches " on a moist surface and then rubbed in with the hand—preferably the latter. " Cheeses bedizened with scarlet require not a blue coat " ; nevertheless the floor of the cheese-room, even when painting was practised, was often prepared with the herbs already mentioned because the herbs were held to keep the rind free from cracks and to protect it from mites. The practice of painting must have endured for my West Country reviewer, as the reader will remember, mentioned it.

It is our misfortune that the literature of Cheese should have been so largely confined to dairy practice. Imagine how large would remain the literature of Wine even if all the technical books on viticulture were left out ! In age cheese is as venerable, for it goes back beyond all tradition. It was familiar to Homer and to the authors of the Old Testament. But, apart from the verses of Thomas Tusser, the English Hesiod of the sixteenth century, from scattered allusions in old ballads, from odd verses or lines in this poet or that prose writer, from

87

"OUR GREAT LOCAL CHEESES ARE DYING."

chapters here and there in our writers of gastronomical books—a good essay by Mr. Belloc,[1] a valuable section by Mr. Morton Shand in his *Book of Food*—these allusions remain to be collected and the English literature of its appreciation to be written. There is perhaps a parable in the fact of Charles Lamb, who says in a letter to Coleridge (November 1802) that " right Gloucester " was his usual supper, explaining that " a crumb, blacked in the candle " marked the passages in his Milton that contained " good matter "; for this seems rather an honour to the poet than to the cheese. Gloucester also has

[1] *First and Last*—By Hilaire Belloc—Essay *On Cheeses*.

a mention in perhaps the most atrocious punning poem of Thomas Hood, the *Epping Hunt*, in which the grocer, John Huggins, stocked " single Glos'ter flat " with round Dutch cheeses.

Because of such neglect and indifference, our great local cheeses are dying. Literature, by preserving the memory and giving the praise of good things, ends by becoming their saviour. We must now therefore resort to it before it is too late. The lovers of English cheese must become vocal, must demand the best, and complain if they do not receive it. Double Gloucester, fully matured, is one of these glories. Its virtue, its history, need to be better known ; for research into the processes of its making are insufficient. Research merely serves the purpose of industry. It is the consumer and appreciator who sets the standard of quality, for that standard faithfully reflects the taste of the market which always bows, in the long run, to the level of the demand.

VII.
LEICESTER

VIII.—LEICESTER CHEESE

By Henry Stevens

Brethren,

The writer calls you this because he hopes that you are "cheese-minded" like himself, but if not he hopes that he may call you "brother-initiates."

The writer was only just grown-up at the end of the Victorian era and even in that short time he has seen huge changes in dietics, many of them beneficial, but others definitely bad.

For example there has been a loss in that taste for cheese (one of the most wholesome of protein foods) which used to distinguish our forebears. The old gentleman of mid-Victorian days had a most discriminating taste in cheese and would treat one of the noble cheeses, such as Wensleydale or Stilton, with the same care and reverence accorded to a bottle of crusted Port.

Now, among the noble cheeses the writer thinks that a definite place may be given to a ripe Cheshire and a Blue Leicester. The more ordinary Leicesters which are factory-made from surplus milk are still unrivalled for the making of toasted cheese or Welsh rarebit; but the farm-made Leicester which is worth maturing with care is, alas, only made in about a dozen farms now.

Cheshire and Double Gloucester both make a good Welsh rarebit, but not so good as the ordinary factory-made Leicester, which is also an excellent luncheon cheese, though not fit for dessert like its aristocratic brother the farm-made Leicester.

The Leicester, in case the reader does not know, is a reddish cheese, rather the colour of Cheshire or Double Gloucester. The colour of these cheeses, like the lips of most ladies nowadays, is admittedly not quite natural, but their sweetness (I mean the cheeses') is unimpaired. In the old days the writer understands that the colour of the Leicester cheese was produced by some extract of carrot, but in these times a vegetable-extract from the Pacific Islands is employed. It is called annatto and is absolutely tasteless and innocuous.

The origin of the Leicester cheese is lost in antiquity, but for centuries past the farmers from every village on the Hinckley, Lutterworth and Market Bosworth sides of Leicester used to send their cheeses in from a radius of twenty miles to the May and October cheese fairs. Frequently the wagoner would have to start before midnight in order to get a good pitch at the fair next morning. These old cheeses were all farm-made and the better ones had a richness and quality never found among the factory-made articles of to-day. The latter is standardised, it is true, but like most standards it is medicore. To-day the cheese fairs are dead and the Leicester cheeses are sold after five or six weeks instead of as many months. All the same the modern Leicester will pay for keeping some weeks longer with a hole punched in the top, a drop of old ale poured into it and a damp cloth over it.

Mr. Tomlinson of Hall Farm, Ullesthorpe, near Rugby, who probably knows as much as any man living about the Leicester cheese, says that as a boy he remembers his father sending cheeses from a village in Warwickshire to the Leicester cheese fairs—the great farm-wagons starting off crack o' dawn, loaded with cheese. In these times you offer the manual worker a bit of raw, colonial cheddar, with about the same flavour as a bit of yellow soap, and he will eat it (with a grimace),

94

FARM WAGON STARTING FOR LEICESTER FAIR.

95

but in Leicestershire, with its great rolling pastures extending into the neighbouring counties and its splendid cattle, you have a bit of England specially designed by Nature for the production of rich, wholesome, nourishing cheese which could be produced as cheaply as the colonial and foreign cheeses and is pleasanter in flavour.

Now let us look at the thing from a national point of view. Cheese provides in its least harmful form the necessary protein for a well-balanced diet. It has hardly any deleterious by-products such as produce thickening of the blood-vessels or nephritis. If only it can be produced in a palatable form and cheaply the public will get educated to it. Leicester cheese may well be the pioneer in this gastronomic revolution. So long, however, as the public have not got beyond associating the word " cheese " with mouse-trap bait we shall not see the solution of some of our economic difficulties. Mr. Tomlinson, before mentioned, says that in the old days the farm-house cheeses were not always " up to sample." The dealers used to come round with special instruments " ironing " the cheeses. This instrument removed a small cylindrical portion of cheese and if this was to be " below Par " in two or three cheeses of one consignment the whole wagon-load might be sent back unsold. This would mean a real tragedy to the unfortunate farmer's wife and daughters who had had many weary hours of work making the cheese. Even with the farm-house Leicester to-day (which can only be obtained at four or five shops in London) one can rely on a more uniform article because of our increased knowledge of moulds, lactic acid, cultures, temperatures, cattle-feeding, etc. A good farm-house Leicester is to-day a great delicacy; it is rich and fat and, when matured, can rank with most ripe Cheshires that one meets in London clubs.

With regard to the making of toasted cheese; Lady Sysonby, in her admirable cook-book, says: " Use either Lancashire Leigh cheese or Canadian Cheddar " ! Oh, heresy ! She goes on to say, " Cut up the cheese into small bits." Now the author solemnly avows, keeping with difficulty to the third person singular, that one gets a much better result with a coarse grater. The result is smoother and less inclined to be stringy. She rightly remarks that only draught ale should be used in this delectable dish and that a tablespoonful of cream for each person should be added besides dusting well with white pepper and adding a level teaspoonful of mustard for each person. Now that tablespoonful of cream just makes all the difference to a toasted cheese made from a factory Leicester. The factory Leicester has not that modicum of cream in its natural state which the farm-made article has. The writer will not tell you about spicing and mulling the draught ale which has to be added as a sort of gravy to be soaked up by the toast. This you must get from Lady Sysonby herself, and you will find it is " the goods."

For Welsh rarebits Mrs. Beeton suggests milk as an alternative to beer for the juice thereof, but to the writer's mind this is but a poor substitute. A chafing-dish is undoubtedly a useful adjunct to the household armament and is admirably adapted to the making of such savouries from Leicester cheese.

Another little point about the making of Welsh rarebit from Leicester cheese : it is quite unnecessary to remove the rind, in fact the flavour is actually better if the rind is grated with the rest. The author remembers the time when, in his youth and innocence, he used to cut off the outside of a Camembert, but it is just as good as the interior and some folk like it better, though he does not recommend the eating of Leicester cheese-rind in the uncooked state.

To revert one moment to the maturing of Leicester cheese. It is important to keep the cloth covering the cheese really damp. It encourages the growth of mould and discourages the breeding of too many mites. The author once possessed a venerable Stilton to which he was sincerely attached, but which developed the extraordinary habit of *purring* like a cat when stroked. Now this sounds preposterous and indeed it was a mystery to the author himself for some time although he won several bets on it from sceptical friends. The explanation was as follows.

The cheese was standing in a cheese-dish that was rather deep like a soup-plate and this permitted a considerable space to exist between the bottom of the cheese and the bottom of the dish. In the course of time a number of the little denizens of the cheese had hatched out into flies, some of which were imprisoned in this space. When the cheese was touched they used to buzz, giving forth a sound exactly like a cat purring. This, one must add, is carrying the ripening process a little *too* far, though not quite so far as that wonderful description of an over-ripe cheese which is to be found in " The Cloister and the Hearth."

It has always been something of a mystery to the writer why Leicester cheese should be classed among the " hard " cheeses. It is really rather a crumbly cheese and should cut quite softly, leaving a creamy smudge on the knife.

Its shape is unusual and has been compared to a mill-stone, much greater in diameter than thickness ; it is therefore very like a Derbyshire cheese in shape.

There are very few shops in London which keep the Leicester cheeses these days, but two of the famous grocers in Piccadilly supply good ones ; certain of the London clubs also keep a Leicester on the " cold table." Leicester cheese is

"LEICESTER CHEESE AND WATERCRESS WERE . . . JUST MADE FOR EACH OTHER."

very popular with the hunting fraternity, and it tastes, if possible, better out of doors than in.

The compiler of this book and the writer of this chapter once sat, side by side, on the banks of what is probably the most beautiful natural spring in the south of England and consumed Leicester cheese with spring onions. A still better mixture is Leicester cheese with those little sweet " pin-money " onions. The spring is a deep turquoise-blue pool about twenty yards by forty, with a chalk bottom covered here and there by forests of emerald-green weeds and inhabited by great old cannibal-trout that cruise about like submarines. The water can be seen bubbling up through about a dozen crevices in

99

"A LIST OF PENALTIES TO BE VISITED ON ANY ONE SELLING
A CHEESE NOT UP TO STANDARD."

the chalk, and the bottom, ten to fifteen feet deep, is in a constant state of turmoil.

The volume of water from this spring is so great that it feeds eight acres of water-cress beds before finally joining the Pang. This brings one to another little gastronomic point; namely, that Leicester cheese and water-cress were just made for each other !

There is another good recipe for Leicester cheese. One takes several slices of bread and just covers them with milk in a fireproof dish. This must be left to soak and then thin slices of cheese are laid on top and thickly spread with mustard and butter. This is put into a quick oven and allowed to brown. This is a most warming dish on a cold winter day, but is too much for a savoury.

The writer must now draw to a close, but may it be a long day before the Leicester cheese is a mere memory like the " Blue Vinny " of Dorset ; even though the cheese market-day in Leicester city is a thing of the past and the Town Crier no longer shouts " Oyez ! Oyez ! Oyez ! " and then recites an imposing list of the awful pains and penalties to be visited upon any one selling a cheese not up to reputed weight or standard.

VIII.
WENSLEYDALE

VIII.—WENSLEYDALE

By Ambrose Heath

As I was about to sit down to write this encomium of what I believe to be the finest of all blue cheeses, there was put into my hand a short essay (or as the author preferred to call it an Exordium[1]) on Cheese, which began as follows: "Some fifty years ago a brother of mine made cheese in Wensleydale, and though his cheese was, to use a Sitwellian phrase, definitely bad, he knew and introduced me to some superb Wensleydale cheese and its quite superb makers. These, alas, are all dead now, and so is superb Wensleydale cheese. There is now no superb Wensleydale. There is only County Council stuff which, though a good deal better than the stuff my brother turned out, has no kind of relationship to the real Wensleydale of fifty years ago. . . . In the times I have spoken of there was a limited quantity of really superb cheese. . . They were made by the old handicraft people, who were themselves, their wives and their daughters and sons bred, born and brought up in real cheese. They smelt of it. They lived it and adored it. Their houses and dairies reeked of it with just the right reek, and if the reek went wrong they knew just what to do. Around and about and among these dear people there lived a large mass of others, who produced a large mass of some edible substance they called cheese. It was terrible stuff. It was cheap and very nasty. There was a

[1] *A brief exordium on Cheese*—C. Rawdon Wood. *Wine and Food No.* 10—Summer Number 1936.

lot of it. The people ate it with onions. It deserved no better fate. Yet it was food. Along came the County Councils and their Cheese Schools. They said, 'Make more and better cheese.' They boosted cheese, and cut out the really bad stuff. What was, however, a tragedy was that they showed that it cost less to produce decent cheese than really fine cheese. The sons and daughters of the old handicraft people went to the new schools and learned what the teachers said. So the fine old aromas and flavours, the product of centuries of care, died out, and only County Council remains to-day."

I have quoted this gentleman at length, because although I cannot claim his age and experience (he speaks of being on the " wrong or ripe side of sixty ") I refuse to believe that there is so great a gap between the cheese of his youth and of mine. One of my earliest memories is that of an aunt and uncle who lived somewhere in Yorkshire—if it was not in Wensleydale, it must have been near—and with whom my father used to stay each year for the grouse-shooting. They were my first introducers to this lovely cheese, for every year there used to arrive two or three brace of birds—and a Wensleydale. It was certainly superb enough for me, and as a cheese has remained so.

And how do I know that my authority's cheese of, say, fifty years ago was actually any better than mine of twenty years later? I was talking one day to that treasury of wisdom, E. V. Lucas, and complaining that the port one drank nowadays, however excellent, never seemed to be as admirable as those glorious vintages of my youth. " But were they really so good, so much better? " he asked. Ah, were they? Was that ecstatic moment of tasting a Jubilee port at another uncle's table, was it any rarer than to-day's young gourmet's thrill of tasting for the first time a port which seems so indifferent to us old 'uns? Wensleydale is so delicious to-day that perhaps it is merely jealousy on the part of us youngsters to deny that it could ever have been more " superb "? A tribute to its excellence was paid the other day by a friend who on hearing that I was to celebrate his favourite cheese, said, " Oh, but you know that the moon is made of green cheese, and the only possible, permissible cheese is Wensleydale! "—an error, nevertheless, because the moon hardly ever looks like a blue cheese, and is much more like the green, and therefore unripe, cheeses which are affected by some Wensleydale-lovers. But no doubt it was in Wensleydale, where tradition and language must always have been cheese, that the saying originated.

That there is still some hope for Wensleydale is expressed at any rate by Mr. Osbert Burdett, whose " *Little Book of Cheese*," published in 1935, is a forerunner of this present volume. He refers to Wensleydale as " the superlative Yorkshire cheese, which is a rival to Stilton in the friendly sense that Bordeaux and Burgundy are sometimes said to be rivals." An acute comparison, this, for there is a quality about Wensleydale which woos the palate (in cheese-eating) in much the same way as claret does. " It would not be possible," says Mr. Burdett, " to savour Wensleydale after Stilton, but it could, perhaps, be eaten before ; though one can understand its wise admirers asserting that it would be shameful to eat any other cheese, green or otherwise, after it. For delicacy, and many would add, for after-savour, the exquisite Wensleydale must receive the crown. . . . Its rare delicacy is becoming better known and it is one of the few local English cheeses which, instead, alas, of dying, has spread its reputation beyond its own county in the past few decades."

Now this is more consoling, and when in the course of my further reading I came across a dictum of that arch-gourmet,

Mr. Morton Shand,[1] to the effect that Stilton cannot be mentioned in the same breath as Wensleydale, the premier cheese of England and one of the world's classic cheeses, I began to think that the precocious predilection of my childhood must have been a very sound one. I felt that perhaps all was not lost with Wensleydale, after all. But my ardour was once more damped on turning over the leaves of a book just published and finding the following : "Except on a few isolated farms the day seems to have gone when the farmers' wives made cheese and butter, and with it has gone some of the romance of the farmhouses when rows of cheese stood in the cheese-rooms and butter and cream on the dairy shelves. But cheese-making, which had to be done every morning from May to September, was heavy work. As soon as the milk came in it was put into a large cheese kettle, heated to a certain temperature and rennet added to separate the curds and whey. In earlier days " keslops," the stomach of a calf pickled and stretched on two sticks to dry, was used instead of rennet. The curds were then kneaded, pressed into moulds and put into cheese presses where they stayed for the night before being placed on the cheese-room shelves to dry. Here they had to be turned daily and the dry ones dusted, a long business as the summer advanced. The process is the same in the dairies, but zinc-lined vats running on wheels have taken the place of the cheese kettles, and the work is a wholetime job. The big dairies can manage their markets better. Cheeses of to-day are often sold new, but the farmer had to wait until late autumn when they had dried and lost weight to sell his, and he had as a rule to accept the shopkeeper's or dealer's price when he came round to bargain for them."[2]

[1] *The Book of Food.*
[2] *Wensleydale*, by Ella Pontefract.

But while the cheese-making industry was passing from the farmer to the dairy, it was the smaller dairies that had a better chance. For the success of the Wensleydale cheese depends, more than anything else, upon the freshness and sweetness of the milk from which it is made, and if the dairy is a very large one the greatest care and supervision of the milk is necessary to ensure a good cheese. According to one authority the precise locality from which the milk has come is an all-important factor. Another declares that while the quality of Stilton depends upon the class of soil and herbage in the district where it is made, no such considerations affect the more accommodating Wensleydale. But let us see how it is made, and what considerations do actually arise.

In its manufacture evening's and morning's milk are used, the evening's milk being cooled to 65° F. directly it has been strained into the vat. In the morning, the skimmed-off cream mixed with some new milk and heated to 90° F. is returned to the vat with the morning's milk, and the starter (that is, milk in which lactic acid bacteria are growing) is added, an ounce to three ounces for every twelve gallons according to the time of the year. The milk is then gradually heated to 84° F. and when 0.18-0.19 per cent of acidity has developed, rennet is added at the rate of one dram to every four gallons of milk. This will make the curd ready for cutting in an hour's time. The correct addition of the rennet seems to be one of the important factors in the making of a good cheese, for the proper flavour of Wensleydale cheese appears to be due, as I have said, not so much to the class of soil and herbage, as to the growth of the blue mould. And this growth depends upon the nature of the curd. If too much rennet is added and coagulation of the milk is too rapid, the result will be bad. For this reason there are still some cheesemakers who contend that home-made rennet is best, because of its slow coagulating properties, and that the best conditions of all are those of the small dairies and farms where temperatures are low and artificial heating is unknown.

When the curd is set it is cut with a widely-set vertical American knife, first lengthways and then across, then left to settle for ten minutes and then cut lengthways with the horizontal knife. It must be kept soft, and stirred as little as possible, but in the initial stages it is stirred gently from the bottom of the vat and allowed to settle for twenty minutes. Stirring then recommences while the temperature is raised gradually to 86° F. When the whey shows 0.13 per cent. of acidity, the curd is left for half an hour or until there is 0.14 per cent. of acidity, and it is then pulled carefully back from the tap end of the vat, and the whey is drawn off. We now begin to get a little nearer our eventual cheese. As soon as the whey has been drawn off, the curd is scooped out into cloths containing enough curd for one cheese. These cloths are on a draining-rack, and they are gently pulled up by their corners so that they form bundles of curd which are in turn covered with more cloths and left on the rack for twenty minutes. After that they are untied, the curd is cut into blocks about four inches square, which are carefully turned and then wrapped up again. This process must be repeated every twenty minutes until the drainings show an acidity of 0.28 to 0.30 per cent., when the curd should be soft and flaky. This will take about three hours. We shall now have, instead of a tough and leathery curd, a soft friable one in which the blue mould should grow luxuriantly. And this is the second difficulty, to be able to develop the right measure of acidity after the rennet has been added. The cheesemaker's skill lies in being able to develop, as an authority says, " just the right amount of

MAKING WENSLEYDALE CHEESE.

III

acidity in the curd so that the drainage overnight will be sufficient. For if the curd drains too much the cheese will be close and tight and resemble a Cheddar ; and if the drainage is not sufficient, the cheeses will ferment on being taken to the curing-rooms and rapidly become discoloured and putrid in the centre." Temperatures must be watched, too, for if the curd becomes chilled, acidity will not develop so well and the cheese will be a badly-flavoured one.

The curd is now broken up, after being weighed, into pieces about the size of walnuts, and then salt is added in the proportion of one ounce of salt for every four pounds of curd. Not until this is thoroughly mixed in and dissolved can the business of moulding and pressing be begun. Then the curd is placed in the unlined moulds loosely and is left to drain without any pressure for a couple of hours. The cheese, as it now is, is next taken out of the mould, turned, wrapped in a cloth and put back into the mould where it must stay for the night in a temperature of 65° F. In the morning it is turned again, the cloth is renewed and it is put in a press with a six-hundredweight pressure for a couple of hours. After that it is taken out, a calico bandage is sewn round it and it undergoes another two hours' pressing. This pressure is light enough not to make the cheese too solid. It is left open in texture in order that it may " blue " later on. " The whole secret," says another authority, "in the manufacture of choice Wensleydale lies in the ability of the maker to determine if the right amount of acidity has been developed at the salting stage. A Wensleydale cheese, if properly made, should be sharp and acid to taste in the earlier stages of ripening, and if in this condition will mould and ripen properly. . . . A Wensleydale cheese when well made and properly ripened is in my opinion the best blue-moulded variety of cheese in the world." And ripening naturally needs great care, best of all perhaps in a cellar; for during this important time high or uneven temperatures of a dry atmosphere are damaging. For the first month or six weeks the cheese is turned every day, and after that every other day. In six months it should be ripe.[1]

And what then? How can I describe that soft rich creaminess? Subtle in flavour as " claret is more delicate than Burgundy." " When ripe " (and this is a hint for discerning shoppers) " the cheese should have a greyish-white skin with the marks of the bandage clearly showing, particularly where the bandage was stitched on. A smooth coat without ridges denotes a hard, acid cheese. A good Wensleydale is soft and flaky, will spread like butter, and has the delicate blue veinings well distributed throughout the curd. The flavour is rich, sweet and creamy—not acid or bitter." There is, too, as I have noted above, an unripened Wensleydale sold, or rather a cheese in the early stages of ripening. But this is flat and weighs less than the usual cheese, and is white, soft and acid, and crumbly. Neither this nor the little creamy cheese known by the trade name of Wenslet compares in any way with the finished glory of the ripened Wensleydale.

And what now? We have peered into the mysteries of its making; what of the rites of consummation? For Wensleydale is no ordinary cheese, to be called for lightly and frivolously as something to fill up the cracks after a thumping good meal, or to take the taste of the sweet away. You will not—or you certainly should not—find a piece of Wensleydale on those wooden boards where Dutch jostles Swiss and goat's milk consorts with cow's. Nor, I hope,

[1]For details of the manufacture of Wensleydale cheese I am indebted to *Cheesemaking*, Bulletin No. 43 of the Ministry of Agriculture and Fisheries and to an article by Mr. John Benson in Vol. XXV. of *The Journal* of the British Dairy Farmers' Association.

will you find your Wensleydale in the same sad state as once I found a Stilton—in a well-known foreign restaurant in London. " But you must have some of our Stilton, m'sieur. It is in the real English style." And after much summoning by waiter and head-waiter, there was borne to me half a Stilton, encased in a kind of bloodstained cloth ; as well it might be, for inside the rind was a strangely lurid pulp which, as he came towards me, the waiter stirred vigorously with a spoon. It was " the real English style," and what had made that caseo-vinous mash was Port! No. To eat Wensleydale is a privilege which must be appreciated keenly. You will recognise your Wensleydale-eaters ; they are kind and gentle souls. Strong hatchet-faced men sit down without a tremor to hunks of Cheddar : the pinkish Cheshire goes well with a certain floridness, the blue with a well-matured complexion that matches so well the glass of port accompanying it. Devotees of Camembert or Brie or Pont-l'Evêque are gay gesticulatory creatures ; those of the rubbery Dutch stiff and stolid ; those of Gruyère and Port Salut rapt in a growing wonder, as if some faint glimmer of the meaning of Cheese might be dawning upon them. This wonder, in pluperfect expression, is the stamp of the Wensleydale-eater. He is now no initiate : the meaning of Cheese in its superexcellence has descended upon him, and with his empty plate before him, having picked up those last few precious crumbs, like Sydney Smith and his Salad he can truthfully say, " I have dined to-day."

And that brings me to another matter. Having chosen your meal, something simple, a soup, a grill and a vegetable, to lead up to the great moment when the Cheese appears, can we like other cheese-eaters take a salad ? For myself I say unhesitatingly, No. Radishes may go admirably with Gorgonzola or celery with Stilton ; a few beautifully selected Cos lettuce leaves may well be considered with the lighter cheeses, and in the outer darkness are those whom hunger or depravity compels to eat onions with Canadian Cheddar. But Wensleydale demands no such supernumeraries. Though stay,—there is a pleasant plant called Corn Salad or Lamb's Lettuce, and in France *Mâche* or *Doucette,* good and prolific in winter, when our Wensleydale comes to us. A succulent and slightly oily leaf it has, vaguely reminiscent of olives. A few plain leaves of this might go with our cheese. I have never tried it ; but it is down in my diary for attempt this year.

And lastly, what are we to drink with Wensleydale ? Port, I think, is too powerful an ally ; besides, it is pledged to Stilton by use. Undoubtedly those two flavours are akin, and I will say nothing to spoil their companionship. André Simon, in his admirable Art of Good Living, gives a list of suggested wines for certain cheeses : a list worth remembering, but alas! he does not mention Wensleydale. " Claret," he writes, " with Gruyère ; Burgundy with Port Salut ; Light Tawny Port with Red Cheshire ; Oloroso Sherry with White Cheshire ; Old Vintage Port with Blue Leicester, and New Vintage Port with Roquefort." I have been thinking all the time of the Blue Wensleydale, of course. The White is another question, and here I should be inclined to agree with Mons. Boulestin who in one of his many books has written that Wensleydale in its early stages is " a perfect background for wines." (And here, in parentheses, if I am not stealing a fellow-essayist's thunder, let me quote an interesting paragraph from Mr. Bunyard's "Anatomy of Dessert": "Sauternes and Pont-l'Evêque cheese should be tried : it will not be the first time that the Church has given the gastronomes a friendly lead.") Well, perhaps Burgundy would do, or even a Claret.

But wine-drinkers must forgive me if I point to what is really the only possible accompaniment : beer. Our English cheeses are brawny, hearty creatures who really need English fashions. A glass of beer comes naturally to the mind—and to the lips! —when cheese is being discussed ; and if your meal is as simple as I have suggested it should be, there is no reason why beer should not after all be best. If you want a dinner where course succeeds course in a growing bewilderment of culinary nomenclature, when carefully-chosen wine follows wine, and all is knit into a delicate pattern of food and drink, in such a meal, if cheese be needed, there is no place for English cheese. They are plain fellows, better suited to a plain oaken table, a clean cloth and a tankard. We shall do no good by trying to dress them up in fancy clothes. But they are great fellows all the same, and worthy to stand up against all comers. And in my humble opinion, the greatest of them is Wensleydale.

That even in these benighted days great cheeses have their devotees may be illustrated by an adventure which befell me a few years ago. I was working at the time in the neighbourhood of one of our great railway stations where there was quite a good restaurant, and thither each day I went for luncheon. Having in due course established congenial relations with the head waiter, I was delighted one day to hear him whisper that he had a particularly good Wensleydale in the restaurant. No second invitation was needed, and when with an air of secrecy (as if this marvel were reserved for his favourite patrons) he bore towards me this noble cheese I knew at a glance that it was " the goods," as he himself informed me. For two or three days this grand procession of the Wensleydale from the sideboard to mewards, and to me only, I noted, continued, and I duly showed my gratitude and appreciation

116

"DON'T YOU KNOW THAT THAT IS A *PRIVATE CHEESE*?"

117

by my helpings. But on the fifth, or was it only the fourth, day my head waiter was not there (it must have been his day off), and as the time of cheese-taking came round my anxiety grew lest I should have to forgo what was now a daily anticipation. Nor was the cheese in evidence. Presently, however, an underling appeared with my darling cheese, and drifted circuitously in my direction. As he did so, I was conscious of another interest than mine. At a neighbouring table there was seated an old gentleman, rather crusty-looking, a retired lawyer, perhaps, I thought, even possibly a Judge—you know the look. And as the Cheese of Cheeses approached my table his interest seemed to deepen. His eyes were riveted on the Wensleydale, and when the waiter stopped by me and I proceeded to help myself, his agitation became almost noticeable. "Another connoisseur of cheeses," I thought comfortably, wondering whether this common interest so naively betrayed might not serve later as an introduction. But he did not look at all benevolent, that old gentleman; and as I raised the first piece of cheese to my lips, I saw his glance of fury, and heard him call out to the waiter, as he passed him, in a loud hiss: "Waiter! Waiter! Dammit, don't you know that that is a *Private Cheese*?"

Now could that have happened to any cheese but a Wensleydale?

IX.

CAERPHILLY

IX.—CAERPHILLY

By Ernest Oldmeadow

A story better known to our Victorian grandfathers than to their Georgian grandsons described the achievement of a resourceful toiler in Grub Street who had accepted a commission to write on Chinese Metaphysics. After skimming the articles on Metaphysics and on China in the current edition of the *Encyclopædia Britannica*, he mended his quill and " combined the information."

Without the guidance of that Victorian scribe's dead hand, I could hardly be sitting myself down in obedience to Sir John Squire's request for " a not very short " paper on Caerphilly Cheese. If the thing is to be spun out over more than a page or two, there will have to be more about Caerphilly than about the small round cakes of white curd which bear that territorial name. But here is one extenuating circumstance. What I shall say will not come out of encyclopædias but out of personal experience.

To associate good food and good drink with favoured spots is a custom as old as literature itself. Take honey. For the ancients, it has to come from Hymettus ; for the moderns, from Narbonne. In due course, owing to the persistent belief that the best things " won't travel," gourmets began to direct their pilgrimages towards gastronomic goals. My memory may be serving me badly, but I recall a Coquelin monologue in which the reciter boasted that he went always to Bresse for a *poularde*, to Rouen for a *caneton*, to Montélimar for his nieces' nougat, to the Rock of Cancale for his oysters, and to Lille—please laugh here—for his *rougets*.

Following admirable examples, I have drunk Pilsener underground in Pilsen, the Hungarian wine called " Bull's Blood " at the vineyard where the blood is yearly shed, Bernkasteler Doktor in the Doktor's own hospitable villa, Château d'Yquem in the spick-and-span chai with the sand-pictures on the floor. That I have also savoured *homard à l'Armoricaine* in Armorica, the lambs of Pauillac within hail of the Château Latour, *omble chevalier* in what was once a monks' refectory on the marge of Lake Annecy, crystallized oranges in the parlour of their original maker at Setubal, Loch Fyne herrings in Ardrishaig, and Danube caviar at Orsova, is nothing to boast about ; but perhaps there has been some light distinction in my lifelong quest of cheese. Even as St. Paul fought with beasts, I have striven with scornful waitresses in Leicester who coldly denied that there is any such thing as Leicester cheese ; and this was not so horrific as what happened at the end of a short ride from the centre of noisy Milan on a tram labelled Duomo-Gorgonzola. But our business is with Caerphilly.

The A.B.C. Railway Guide shows that Caerphilly is 152 miles distant from Paddington and that it can be reached in 215 minutes. But the thing to do is to make for Cardiff. That this great city, the most important in all Wales, remains unknown to scores of thousands of Englishmen who have seen nearly all the great towns in Europe is a lamentable fact. Cardiff's monumental group of public buildings, national and municipal, is one of the finest architectural ensembles in the British Isles ; and the city's big show-places, from the old Castle to the new Museum, are of real importance.

Instead of using the begritted Rhymney railway for the short journey from Cardiff to Caerphilly it is best to take the

122

motor-bus, which usually carries an interesting medley of short-stage passengers. About half an hour after leaving the Castle of Cardiff, the Castle of Caerphilly comes into sight; and it is a sight indeed. Few are the tears that I could squeeze out for the man who has never tasted Welsh cheese; but they could flow freely for him who has not seen the greater Welsh castles. Conway, with its almost unbroken oblong of mediæval round towers and corbelled walls, has been glimpsed by many a headlong traveller on his way to Ireland; and Carnarvon, one of the most imposing piles in all Britain, has been made familiar by pictures of the investiture therein of the Prince of Wales. Harlech, too, has looked down from its proud height on thousands of visitors to the bathing-places on Cardigan Bay. But Kidwelly (which does not rhyme with Dolgelly but is pronounced as in English) and Pembroke and Caerphilly are known to few, although they are far bigger than Conway and Carnarvon and Harlech. Caerphilly spreads over thirty acres of ground, while Carnarvon covers only three. Perhaps Caerphilly was in Dr. Johnson's mind when, after his tour of the Hebrides, he said that " the ruins yet remaining of some one of the castles the English built in Wales" would "find materials " for all the castles he had seen beyond the Tweed.

Lest readers whom these lines may some day turn into Caerphillian pilgrims be disappointed, I make haste to say that Caerphilly Castle, though vast and though full of points for the antiquary and for the military engineer, is not the most amiable of our homeland ruins. Unlike such castles as Edinburgh's, which crown picturesque and almost precipitous heights, Caerphilly Castle rises only a few feet above the marsh which was its most formidable defence; and, through its lack of trees and ivy, its ruins are stark. Even on an August afternoon, I have been more glad to find shelter there from bleak wind than shade from glaring sun. At the expense of its owner, the Marquis of Bute, costly works of repair and restoration are in progress. This is not the place for discussing the sharp criticisms which have been directed against the architect employed by the noble Marquis; but it is necessary to warn intending visitors that the newness of the masonry aggravates the starkness of these remains. None the less—perhaps rather the more for its harshness—Gilbert de Clare's mighty stronghold has its own grim fascination. The Inner Ward, with a round tower at each angle, is about two hundred feet in length and almost as broad as it is long. But the chief glory of Caerphilly Castle was the lordly " Great Hall," now sufficiently roofed and cleansed to serve as a refectory for hundreds of trippers at a time. They eat at trestle-tables, and their snack meals do not bring into action the unique old kitchen where once were roasted the birds and beasts for the banquets of princes and nobles. As I did not have the happiness of visiting the Great Hall at the trippers' feeding-time, I am not able to say how much or how little Caerphilly cheese was in their bags and baskets. The other glory of Caerphilly Castle is the " Grand Front," an outwork 800 feet long. By damming a tributary of the Rhymney River, the old English builders protected the Castle on every side with lakes and moats, while the fortress itself consisted of enormously massive stonework. It is instructive to contrast Caerphilly's concentric plan with the lay-out at Pembroke, where the site presented the builders with a quite different set of architectural and military problems.

In that part of Caerphilly town where one waits for the 'bus, I was heavily depressed. The shops were of the type which, by their ugly window-dressing and their dogged preference for standardisation, do more than anything else to rob industrial towns of such individuality as is within their grasp. The

" YE OLDE SHOPPE."

provision stores were displaying " Canadian Cheddar "; but I saw no Caerphilly. Nor did my eye detect anywhere the expected " Original Shop " which is almost always to be found in an old place—by the way, Caerphilly is a market town as well as a colliery centre—where some famous dainty has a local habitation and a name. Wherever there is a renowned make of pork pies or sausages or black-puddings or cakes or toffee, the itinerant epicure counts upon finding in the market-place (or the High Street or Church Lane) some timber'd and gabled and low-ceiling'd establishment called " Ye Olde

Shoppe," where the town speciality is said to be made and sold by the exclusive heirs to the primal recipe. Nor is he surprised or discouraged when, on the opposite side of the market-place (or the High Street or Church Lane), he comes upon a second " Olde Shoppe " making the same claim and perhaps even urging strangers to be on their guard against imitators and upstarts. It may be that Caerphilly is likewise furnished. If so, I did not chance upon the Shoppe. Nor did I even encounter an enterprising shopkeeper, like those in Chester City and in Cheddar Village who are always ready to sell you a baby Cheshire or a miniature Cheddar. It is true that there are hotels in Caerphilly, notably " The Clive Arms " and " The King's Arms," where one might reasonably hope to find Glamorgan cheese keeping company with Glamorgan ale ; but, as my stay in the town synchronised with the rigidly observed closing-hours, I could not test the local patriotism of these establishments.

In populous and progressive Cardiff, I fared little better than in small and depressed Caerphilly. Here is an abridgement of the sorry little story as I have already tried to tell it in another place.[1] Before going from Cardiff to Caerphilly, I ate an early and excellent luncheon in a sumptuously fitted restaurant, where waitresses, not waiters, took one's orders. At the outset of the meal and throughout its progress, my own particular Hebe revealed considerable and even exceptional intelligence ; so it was with confidence that I asked, after the sweets, for Caerphilly cheese. Hebe laughed. Evidently she thought that it was my little joke ; as if I had asked a Piccadilly waiter for Piccadilly cheese or a Lyons waitress for a cheese made from lionesses' milk. Cheddar and Camembert she offered to me ; also a Danish-looking Roquefort and some

[1] In No. 1 of the delightful little quarterly *Wine and Food*, 1934

"STRIVEN WITH SCORNFUL WAITRESSES."

tiny wedges of unholey Gruyère, wrapped up in silver paper. But no Caerphilly. Remembering the migratory habits of Britain's *post bellum* population, I suspected that this young woman was probably not Cardiff-born but perchance a Cornish girl, or a Cockney, or an emigrée from County Durham. I asked if she had ever heard of Caerphilly. She retorted briskly that she " ought to of," seeing that her own father had been born there. But when I pleaded " Surely you know there is Caerphilly cheese," she answered, with a toss of the head that, no doubt, there was " plenty of cheese in the Caerphilly shops, the same as everywhere else." Not being a Defeatist, I told the damsel that I would be lunching on the morrow at the same table and at the same hour, in the hope of eating a choice morsel of Caerphilly cheese. The morrow came ; but not the cheese. Expostulation finally brought the manager in person to my table. He admitted that Caerphilly town was only half a dozen miles away and that it did indeed give its name to a cheese; but he assured me paternally that I " wouldn't like it "; that " nobody ever asks for it "; and that, the last time he had bought it for the restaurant, " most of it went bad."

A few hours later, I partly fathomed the restaurateur's difficulty. Before leaving Cardiff, I had rescued and borne away a wee wedge of Caerphilly cheese which had been sitting forlorn on a Cardiff grocer's counter amidst cliffs and bastions of Cheddar and pseudo-Cheddar. It turned out to be not worth eating. Although Caerphilly is usually classed among what are called the hard-pressed kinds of cheese, it needs to be consumed quickly. Indeed, a Caerphilly kept more than a very short time makes mock of the clumsy old proverb about the difference between chalk and cheese; because it resembles both those substances, with the chalk as predominant partner.

If these experiences of mine be not abnormal, how shall we account for the waning of Caerphilly's vogue on its native heaths? One reason is that the big factory-made cheeses which are mass-produced in the U.S.A. and in certain British Dominions are usually a little cheaper than Caerphilly, and that, being of the Cheddar type, they are more satisfying to ordinary stomachs. When toasted or melted, they are seen to be more fat than the Glamorgan product and are therefore considered to be much better value for money. Further, their countrified buttercup colour appeals to eyes which are not attracted by the anæmic paleness of Caerphilly. It has also been argued in my hearing that Glamorgan and Monmouth now hold a serious percentage of Irish-bred inhabitants and that Ireland, though one of the most favoured of Europe's dairy-countries, has not produced a race of cheese-eaters. By this argument I am not deeply impressed. More convincing is

128

the fact that the production of Caerphilly cheese has largely shifted from South Wales to other centres. A London cheese-monger who sells every year hundreds of tons of divers cheeses recently told me that a bit of his Caerphilly, which I had praised as exceptionally good, came from Leicestershire and not from Glamorgan or any other Welsh shire. He added, however, that the managers of the Leicestershire establishment were Welshmen. He told me further that a cheese of Caerphilly style came to him not long ago from Ulster but that he could not sell it after the first few weeks. True Caerphilly, he said, is " the best cheese for weak stomachs." The Ulster imitation was found " too good," in the sense of being too creamy. And this brings me, at long last, to Caerphilly cheese itself.

If I had to describe Caerphilly cheese in a single sentence to readers who do not already know its bouquet and flavour I might say that, when in perfect condition, it is an almost ideal cheese for those who love buttermilk, and that those who hate buttermilk had better leave it alone. Some of us enjoy buttermilk in copious draughts. At a Cheshire farm-house on an August afternoon, buttermilk in a blue-and-white mug is both nectar and ambrosia. Yet I have drunk it—two beakers in succession—with equal delight on a March night, in a peoples' milk-bar in chilly Glasgow. I know, however, that there are men and women much better than I am to whom buttermilk and yaghourt, *et id genus omne* are anathema. To all such I say that they can make a better use of this short life than to go a-hunting after Caerphilly cheese.

The Caerphilly (or Leicester-Caerphilly) cheese which I have lately been buying is shaped into round loaves weighing six pounds each. As each cheese requires only about four gallons of milk, and as there is no locking-up of capital through long storage and maturing, Caerphilly ought never to be very dear. The best of my recent purchases in this line cost only eightpence a pound, but buyers of small quantities ought not to jib at a shilling. Even at eightpence, however, the stuff will be dear to cheese-lovers who do not know how to treat this breed of domestic pet. The best method is to wet an old table-napkin under the cold tap and to wring it out as much as possible. The cheese ought to be wrapped in this; and when the cloth gets quite dry it should again be made damp. I say damp. Not wet. As a wrapping for a good piece of not very old Cheshire, I smear a sheet of kitchen paper (grease-proof) with butter and I take care that the buttered side of the paper adheres closely to every inch of the Cheshire; but this would not do for Caerphilly.

As for the eating of Caerphilly cheese, far and away the best use of it is with a crisp roll, as a simple finish to luncheon. I know a man who cuts a neat slice, rather less than half an inch thick, and eats it like a piece of cold meat, with a knife and fork, after first trimming away the delicate rind. Sometimes he associates it with a small portion of salad—the whitest and curliest and crispest parts of a fresh lettuce, lightly dressed with oil and vinegar. Sliced very thinly indeed—an operation to which Caerphilly lends itself gracefully—it can be laid between superfine slices of white or brown bread-and-butter to which a very little mustard has been applied with a stippling touch. Two or three sandwiches having been thus made and placed one on top of another, the pile is held down firmly while the crusts are pared off with a sharp knife, and they are then packed up, even if one does not want them for a picnic, in a damp cloth until the moment of serving. Dryness, either in the cheese itself or in its accompaniments, is disastrous to Caerphilly.

It sounds horribly messy to suggest mashing with a fork

tiny pieces of Caerphilly in a tablespoonful of beer ; but this is easily done in a soup-plate. The mess is then cooked gently in a small enamelled saucepan, stirring until it is smooth and piping hot. It must be consumed straight away, with a little more beer to help it down. Although this austere dish is certainly not a dainty, it makes a nourishing and easily digested supper, once in a way, for those who dare not eat much just before bedtime but cannot sleep on an empty stomach. Small squares of buttered toast should accompany the hot cheese.

For a *Fondue Caerphilly*, it is better to depart from the Brillat-Savarin proportions of weight. Weigh the eggs—one for each person—and allow an almost equal weight of Caerphilly, cut up as finely as apple parings. Supposing that two eggs together weigh five ounces, add four ounces of the cheese and one ounce and a half of butter. These proportions are very different from those given in the French cookery-books for a classical fondue, but it must be remembered that the classical dish is made with Gruyère. Beat the eggs as for an omelette ; that is to say, until yokes and whites are blended together but without frothing. Put eggs, cheese and butter in a saucepan and cook the mixture rather quickly, stirring it without cease. Towards the end of the process, the contents of the saucepan will thicken. At this point the Brillat-Savarin rule must be strictly obeyed and the stiffening must be arrested the moment the fondue has become thick enough to be eaten with a fork instead of with a spoon. At the last moment, the stirring-in of a teaspoonful of freshly-made mustard may be an improvement. Serve the mess along with (not on) nicely buttered toast and with a glass of good Burgundy or half a pint of stout for each guest. But, so that nobody may be disappointed, I say again that the Caerphilly palate is a buttermilk palate and that those epicures who dote upon Welsh rarebits made from

131

good Cheshire and on *fondues* made from Gruyère will not think highly of my Fondue Caerphilly.

What it all comes to is that, as the French say, the Best is the enemy of the Good. Caerphilly will annoy those narrow persons who sulk whenever an experiment in the gastronomic field causes them to spend part of the day's precious appetite on something which, though it be novel, is less delicious than some much more famous rival in the same class. But he who is gourmet rather than glutton will find Caerphilly well worth attention, now and then; while the devotees of buttermilk will not be sure that there is any cheese which they like better.

At the outset of this paper, a promise was given that personal experience rather than excerpts from books should furnish it. But candour compels the admission that this was a case of Hobson's choice. The cheese of Caerphilly has lacked its minstrels.

"Surely you forget," said a friend to whom I had bewailed Caerphilly's unsungness, "that there is a chapter in Borrow." Having indeed forgotten it, I made haste to turn it up. It is Chapter CVII. of Wild Wales and is duly headed "Caerfili." But there is not one word in it about the local or any other cheese. The omission is instructive; because George Borrow was a pioneer of regional gourmandise. Many a mouth has watered at his account of the "noble breakfast" eaten at the long-famous and still excellent White Lion, in Bala—the breakfast which included "tea and coffee, a goodly white loaf and butter, a couple of eggs and two mutton chops, broiled and pickled salmon, fried trout, potted trout or potted shrimps." As for his regional sense, it comes out strongly in this note on a dinner in furnished lodgings at Llangollen:

" We had salmon and leg of mutton ; the salmon from the Dee, the leg from the neighbouring Berwyn. The salmon was good enough, but I had eaten better ; and here it will not be amiss to say that the best salmon in the world is caught in the Suir, a river that flows past the beautiful town of Clonmel in Ireland. As for the leg of mutton, it was truly wonderful ; nothing so good had I ever tasted in the shape of a leg of mutton. The leg of mutton of Wales beats the leg of mutton of any other country. . . . Certainly I shall never forget the first Welsh leg of mutton which I tasted, rich but delicate, replete with juices derived from the aromatic herbs of the noble Berwyn, cooked to a turn and weighing just four pounds. . . . Let any one who wishes to eat leg of mutton in perfection, go to Wales, but mind you to eat leg of mutton only. Welsh leg of mutton is superlative : but, with the exception of the leg, the mutton of Wales is decidedly inferior to that of many other parts of Britain."

I grant, though grudgingly, that a man may know good mutton without knowing good cheese ; but there is another page in *Wild Wales* where Borrow shows that good cheese was one of his pursuits. At Chester he fondly said :

" I shall have a treat in the cheese. Cheshire cheese has always been reckoned excellent : and, now that I am in the capital of the cheese-country, of course I shall have some of the very prime . . .

" To my horror the cheese had much the appearance of soap of the commonest kind, which indeed I found it much resembled in taste, on putting a small portion into my mouth. ' Ah,' said I, after I had opened the window and ejected the half-masticated morsel into the street, ' those who wish to regale on good Cheshire cheese must not come to Chester, no more than those who wish to drink first-rate coffee must go to Mocha.'"

With these sapient examples of Borrovian gastrology in mind, the reader of *Wild Wales* tramps down the Rhymney Valley in the hungry George's company, expecting a noteworthy pronouncement on Caerphilly cheese. Chapter CVI. concludes with this promising sentence :

"I reached Caerfili at about seven o'clock, and went to the Boar's Head, near the ruins of a stupendous castle on which the beams of the moon were falling."

Next day Borrow explored and admired the ruins. But, instead of tasting the cheese, to bless or to curse it, he went off on one of those excursions into dictionary-philology for which he fondly believed he had a true scholar's fitness. Spelling the place-name " Caerfili," he declared that it is " called so after one Philip, a saint." Whether the large unlovely town on the Nant-y-Gledyr be indeed " called after " a saint, few, if any, of us know ; but we do know that a cheese is " called after " Caerphilly, and it is a dismal thought that our illustrious and loquacious amateur of cheese slept there more than fourscore years ago without seeing it, smelling it, tasting it, or even hearing one word about it.

But, lest the reproachful shade of mine host at the " Boar's Head " cry out against an injustice, we are bound to admit that Borrow, on that moonlight night just after the battle of Inkerman, may have eaten Caerphilly cheese without knowing its provenance. So hefty a trencherman, entering his inn after seven hours of tramping through November air, would not go dinnerless to bed. So much cash remained in his purse that, only a night or two later, he " engaged a private room and ordered the best dinner the people could provide " in Chepstow's principal inn, where he paid a reckoning (including a bottle of port) " amounting to something considerable." So who can say that a chunk of mute inglorious Caerphilly did not end the " Boar's Head's " unwritten menu ? M. Jourdain's is a widespread family. I myself have met a lady who, for many years, ate and relished an enviable Double Gloucester from a small and most honourable dairy ; but she did not know she was eating Gloucester. She knew only that she was eating cheese.

X.
DUNLOP

X.—DUNLOP CHEESE

By Moray M'Laren

Dunlop is not an English cheese : it is Scotch. Here let me pause to meet the indignation which the sight of that word may arouse in the minds of my compatriotic readers. There is, surely (and for some reason which I cannot explain, but with which I sympathise), nothing wrong with the word Scotch when it is applied to edibles and drinkables, while it is offensive when used about persons, poems, songs, music and things of the mind and heart generally. Scottish whisky is as ridiculous as Scotch man is unpleasant. The Editor of this book is certainly the most convinced and convincing Englishman living; and it was indeed kind of him to include in a book on English cheese a Scotch one. I feel, however, that at the beginning of this contribution I must make quite clear the nationality of Dunlop.

There is a certain necessity in doing this ; for if Dunlop goes from Scotland, all is lost, including honour. Dunlop is the only Scotch cheese. There are, it is true, stories about certain small local and individual cheeses having been made in the farmlands of Aberdeenshire and maybe in Orkney ; but none of them have really emerged sufficiently into the light for the cheese-lover to recognise them. There is, of course, the substance known as crowdie, but while it is agreeable, one cannot count it as a cheese. The old Highland system of living produced a world-famous drink and some curious dishes about which Miss Marian MacNeill has written learnedly and on

"THE OLD SYSTEM OF LIVING PRODUCED A WORLD-FAMOUS DRINK."

which that great Scottish cook, Mrs. Christine Roebuck of Edinburgh, has experimented. But there was no cheese in the Western Hills and Islands.

If you take Great Britain as a whole, cheese is undoubtedly an English product. And it is easy to understand this. " Sir," said one of the greatest of all Englishmen, speaking to his Scottish biographer, " we have more of the sun than you have ; our land is richer, our blood thicker." The taste of cheese, the very sound of the word recalls the image of rich pasture land, meadows, slow-flowing streams—the English scene. The Scottish background, while it is astonishingly varied, does not contain much of that particular kind of richness. Its moorlands with their grouse and deer, its green hills on which browse the sheep that produce the finest mutton in the world (fit accompaniment to the traditional Scottish importation of claret), its rivers and burns with their superb sea trout, salmon and trout, its herring haunted coasts, its honey-producing heather, its oatmeal, its remote farms where the mistress can bake scones that cannot be beaten all the world over—all these will provide great delight for the traveller in Scotland who " minds his belly." Save for Dunlop, however, the Scottish scene will not produce for him cheese. It is understandable, but at the same time, it is a pity and it is strange. It is a pity because the best of Scottish food and cooking comes from just that domestic and farmhouse background which, in other countries, has produced cheese. It is strange because the greatest country in the world for cheeses (I am bold enough to say this despite the title of this book) is France. One would have thought that the old friendship, which influenced the Scottish tongue so much, which set the style of Scottish architecture, which was responsible for certain still-surviving elements in the Scottish cuisine, might have inspired the people of Scotland to develop their own cheeses. However, the only appreciable effect that the French love of cheese has had on Scotland has been to give the average travelling Scot an almost insatiable appetite for the lovely and varied cheeses of that land.

Dunlop is, of course, an Ayrshire cheese. Any one who knows about cheeses and who has travelled in Scotland will understand why ; one look at the lowlands of Ayrshire will suffice. It has often been remarked that, despite the popular view that Scottish scenery is entirely composed of wild and romantic views of hills and mountains, Scotland does contain within its small boundaries an extraordinary variety of scene. There are the sharp, clear-cut, cold Lowlands of the East and the red lands of East Lothian, the farm country of Buchan and Aberdeen, the strange no-man's-land of the Borders, the wastes and desolation of the far North, the domestic Highlands of Galloway, the unexpected arable land of Orkney, the fantastic beauty of the West Highlands, and, for the purpose of Dunlop cheese, the rich land around Ayr.

This country is, to the casual observer, possibly the least Scottish of all land in Scotland. And those who, because they knew that Robert Burns is the poet of Scotland, have always seen him in their imagination against a background of the " mountain and the flood," must have been surprised when they visited for the first time his native countryside and noted its almost exotic qualities—exotic as far as the popular conception of Scotland goes.

The coast of Ayrshire runs almost the whole length of the Firth of Clyde after the river turns south. The hills do not come down to the sea, but for the most part lie well back, allowing a rich and fertile plain to lie sheltered between it and the wild channel of water that runs down to Ireland and the Atlantic. On the other side of the Firth of Clyde there are the hills of Arran and the long projection of the Mull of Kintyre. To the south-west there is Ireland, and to the north again there are hills to protect the country from cold winds. With the exception of parts of Galloway, this country is probably the warmest in Scotland. Its hills are round and green. Its rivers are a compromise between the turbulence of Scottish burns and the placidity of English streams ; they have long stretches of slow-flowing water, and in summer the thickly-leaved branches of trees hang over them in much the same way as they do over the canal-like waters of the South. There are some fine eighteenth-century houses, built in the domestic and not in the baronial manner. There is park land, and there are farms, rich and well founded. The moorland of the larger hills on which grouse abound lies well back and is not a part of the domestic countryside of Ayrshire. It is a garden wall— and a very agreeable one at that.

It is in such circumstances that Scotland's only cheese has been produced. Mr. R. Hedger Wallace says (my authority is Mr. Osbert Burdett) that, " according to a tombstone at Dunlop, these cheeses were first made in the time of King Charles II. by Barbara Gilmour, who learnt how to make such cheeses in Ireland." This Barbara Gilmour introduced the habits of making sweet milk cheese from Ireland, whence she had been driven at the time of the religious troubles. The statistical account of Scotland in 1793 in its reference to the parish of Dunlop confirms this story of its origin and adds that the grandson of Barbara Gilmour was still living at that date and was the proprietor of the farm, carrying on the production of the cheese.

The making of Dunlop cheese flourished in the eighteenth and nineteenth centuries and, of course, it can still be got to this day, though what with the creameries and the marketing boards, it seems like so many good things to be on the way to disappearance. It is still common enough, though much of it still called Dunlop is not quite the genuine article.

Mr. James Fergusson of Kilkerran tells me that twenty years ago all the farms in his part of the world used to make it as a matter of course, and that as a boy he remembers that the size and shapes of the cheeses he used to see regularly at the farms at Kilkerran made them look like Stiltons, though of course, the colour was quite different. He was recently lamenting the fact that few of these farms now make it independently. Most of them, alas ! send their milk to factories for the production of a cheese which is by no means the same stuff.

It was the same Mr. Fergusson who first introduced me to Dunlop cheese at the New Club, Edinburgh—that home of all good Scottish edibles and drinkables—and I remember arguing with him on that occasion about Dunlop and its rival Cheddar.

"MADE THEM LOOK LIKE STILTONS . . . AT THE FARMS AT KILKERRAN."

At the time, my palate had not quite accustomed itself to the subtlety of the Dunlop taste and I put it a little bit below Cheddar. It is the consistency of Cheddar and in colour is between butter and cream. I have eaten it frequently since then, and now agree that it is sweeter than its Southern kind. It is smoother, has less bite, is not so painful on the gums and does not dry the mouth so forcibly. Though some who eat it like it old, I much prefer it fresh. But no one should go away with the notion that because it is agreeable when fresh and because I have praised it for its smoothness and lack of bite, that Dunlop cheese is merely a piece of dull solidified milk, to

144

be appreciated only by those simple palates that are repelled by the rich complexity of taste in more Southern cheeses. The civilised eater of cheeses should be able to appreciate both kinds. There is a charm in the fresh complexion of the country girl just as there is art and beauty in the *maquillage* of the Parisienne.

Cheese such as Dunlop takes its place amongst those quiet but none the less subtle foods which provide some of the best portions of the Northern table. Heaven forbid that all cheeses should be like Dunlop ! Even the enthusiast for plain cooking must occasionally wish for a little gastronomic adventure. For myself, after I have enjoyed even the best of Northern cooking for some weeks, I suffer a keen nostalgia for the sauces and spices of the French style—the sauces and spices with which a French housewife can, one almost believes, make an old boot delightful to eat. Nevertheless, the quiet style has its place and, after a surfeit of richness, one longs to return to it for a while.

Though Dunlop cheese is simple, it has its nuances and its excellences. Think of the other kinds of food which are on the tables and sideboards which it decorates with its presence. Imagine a meal in which it has its place. Sit down to this : a small plateful of not too thickly cooked broth (with a touch of pepper added in serving), with the broth a dry sherry ; grilled sea trout or brown trout from the river cooked with oatmeal ; then saddle of mutton with new potatoes and possibly (though this is a liking of my own which all may not share) some leeks served on another plate ; with the mutton a pint of good claret, or, if you are not sure of getting claret that is quite up to standard, some really good ale from the barrel and served in a tankard will do. To end up with (if you do not want any sweets, and I do not think you had better want any) some oatcakes and Dunlop cheese. With the cheese drink the best claret you have or finish up the ale. But whatever you do, avoid port. It is a rich, sweet, English drink, delightful in its right place, but offensive at the end of such a meal.

Those who enjoy such food, who love the delicate succulence of good mutton, who prefer claret to burgundy, sea trout to salmon, herring to halibut, will like Dunlop cheese and will hear with regret of its departure from the farm produce of Ayrshire.

It is, alas! so characteristic of what is going on at the present time, that so quiet and charming a product of country art and tradition as this local cheese should be one of the things to be caught up in the factory system. Such strong and noble cheeses as Stilton, Double Gloster and the like have so imprinted their taste on the palates of the gourmets that there will always be enough enthusiasts to see and insist that somewhere the genuine stuff is being produced. The French have, of course, far too much sense and taste to allow their famous cheeses to be corrupted, and would no more think of letting them lose their individuality than they would allow their wines to be produced by artificial processes. But with us it is different. The small, the quiet, the local, the traditional, in the way of eating and drinking, is being absorbed into the machine. Our beer too often comes out of the chemist's retort, our cheese out of the factory press. " What does it matter," cries your impatient progressivist, " if it tastes just as good, where it comes from ? " And the tragedy is that he thinks it does taste just as good. You cannot argue about such things.

What you can argue about, however, is this. The cultivation and preservation of what the French call " spécialités régionales " is the very essence of gastronomy. If you look at the country of France on the map of the world, how small it

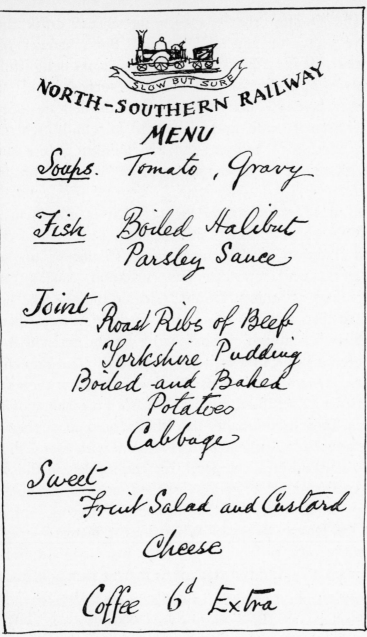

NORTH-SOUTHERN RAILWAY

SLOW BUT SURE

MENU

Soups. Tomato, Gravy

Fish   Boiled Halibut
        Parsley Sauce

Joint   Roast Ribs of Beef
        Yorkshire Pudding
        Boiled and Baked
        Potatoes
        Cabbage

Sweet
        Fruit Salad and Custard

        Cheese

Coffee 6ᵈ Extra

seems, and though it is a large country, it occupies only a small portion of the map of Europe. Yet not only is France the home of the best cooking and the best wines in the world, but it contains a greater variety of eating and drinking than any other part of the surface of the globe. Not every one has had the pleasure of travelling leisurely through France by foot or by motor-car, but most people who have been abroad have, at one time or another, had their lunch in the North of France, their dinner in Paris, their lunch the next day in the Midi and their dinner in the South. Those four meals will show a variety of cooking and of pleasure that (if the traveller chooses carefully) cannot be beaten anywhere else in the world.

Superficially, the French have adopted as much of the mass-produced pleasures of America as any other country in Europe. Their cinemas are luxurious and up-to-date ; the sports cars that stream up and down the long, straight, ugly French roads are as enormous as elsewhere ; nowadays the old gibe at the Frenchman not liking hot water and baths is dead—the average French hotel has more modern and elaborate conveniences for pleasurable bathing than the average English one ; the aeroplane is as frequent there as anywhere else, and all modern ways of getting about and enjoying oneself are certainly not less in France than in England or even America. But underneath all this there is a conservatism about the things that matter, which France will never lose, and one of the most important of these is conservatism in pleasures of the table. Each province, each town, each district—almost each village— has its own special product or special way of cooking that product. A man would need the fortitude of an ox and the life of a giant tortoise to eat his way through France and to consume every " specialité " that could be produced for him.

All arguments about food eventually have to come back to France and I imagine that there will be other references to the cuisine of that country in this book of cheeses. I know, however, how dangerous and often how fruitless it is to keep on belabouring our own table by comparing it with the excellences of the French one. I know, also that when you are talking about so small, sea-girt and Northern a country as Scotland, comparison with the rich, warm and fruitful land of France is especially dangerous. But the one thing the whole of this island of Great Britain does not lack is variety, and if there is one place where that variety is found at its most startling and in the smallest compass, it is the Northern end. Within half a day's motor journey from Edinburgh, you can see a variety of scenery and a quality of land that can hardly be rivalled, in my experience, elsewhere in Europe. We are constantly being told that people's habits and qualities are affected not only by climate but by the scenery in which they live. Surely then, it is not too much to expect that this country should have produced a variety of dishes to eat and to drink. It is true that in the past, the variety, if not large, was at least full-flavoured. The land of cakes was not called so without any reason, and to this day if you like sweet things (I am afraid I do not) you will get the best and as wide a variety of cakes, jams, preserves and other homely dishes of that kind in Scotland as elsewhere. The ordinary ways, however, of cooking meats and fish remain ordinary and, alas ! for the most part unchanged all over the country. What makes them excellent is the fact that the meat is admirable, that it is simply cooked and that it is served fresh.

Apart, therefore, from these admirable meats, these occasional ways of cooking oatmeal and flour, amongst the only true " specialités régionales " which Scotland has produced, the Dunlop cheese is the foremost, yet it is disappearing. If you ask for Dunlop at any average Scotch hotel, they will probably not know what you mean. If the hotel is in Ayrshire, they might. If you ask for it at any grocer of any size, they will produce it for you, but the odds are that it is factory-made and has probably never been near Dunlop and is lucky if it has seen Ayrshire. If you are persistent, however, and demand from your shop or agent that the cheese should really come from a farm ; if, moreover, you have the taste to perceive, when you eat it, whether or not your agent is telling the truth, you will then be fortunate enough to enjoy the real thing. How long this will go on one cannot say. Possibly the interest which the Editor of this book is striving to arouse in cheese throughout the United Kingdom may help to keep this one cheese of Scotland alive. Possibly man's natural disgust at the mechanisation of life may be just in time to save it amongst the other important details of our native table.

In the meantime, it is sad to see such a decline taking place in Scotland. Whatever are the faults of our strange country, the discarding of tradition has not so far been one of them. Indeed, we have often been taunted with an obstinate conservatism in retaining little things which, to our Southern neighbours, have seemed unimportant.

Perhaps this is being too pessimistic. But it is difficult not to be pessimistic about certain culinary matters nowadays. Perhaps I have been misled about the extent of the decline of farm-produced Dunlop. Indeed, I am pretty well sure I have. Any one who knows the Scottish countryside knows that nothing there is quite as it seems on the surface. There must be some quiet Ayrshire farms where the real Dunlop is still being made and will continue to be made a fit companion in remote houses and homes to those other ornaments of the Scottish table, for which, thank God ! no factory can make substitutes—our mutton, our trout, our salmon and our game.

XI.
IRISH

XI.—IRISH CHEESES

By Oliver St. J. Gogarty

During the years 1914 to 1918, when food of every kind was in demand, much cheese was made in Ireland, but some of it was hastily produced and of a poor quality. Mr. Hogan, one of the most competent men Ireland has produced, came into office in 1922 as Minister of Agriculture. He set about a reformation of our dairies so that they might compete successfully with the Danish dairies. With a richer, more fertile and sheltered soil than Denmark, merely a matter of technique stood between the excellence of our dairy products and those of Denmark. For years our experts had been highly trained and efficient, but acts of Parliament were required to control the dairies and to standardise their workings. When this was at last accomplished, the experts were sent round to instruct the dairymaids, and leaflets were broadcast.

The story goes that when application was made to Denmark for an instructor to teach the Irish the art of butter and cheese production and preservation, the Danish authorities apologised for being unable to lend their best expert " because he had just gone back to Cork ! "

As in England, the great dairy farms of Ireland are in the south-west. Out of Cork the expert and his colleagues must have issued in force, because to-day the dairies of Ireland are producing some of the most wholesome and nutritious cheeses in the world : 2,521,141 lbs were sold last year. This is as it should be, because no country on earth is so peculiarly endowed

by Nature or more likely to overflow with milk and honey as this unhibernating Hibernia of ours.

For a while the cheeses we produced were called after English prototypes—" Irish " Cheddar, " Irish " Stilton. Now that these types are established they are called after the native places of manufacture : Ardagh, Galtee, Whitethorn, etc.

Here is a list of the principal cheese-producing dairies : Ballyroe, Newmarket, Freemount, Knockavardagh, Herbertstown, Lissarda, Effin, Kilmallock, Milford, Dungarvan, Suirvale, Experimental Dairy University College, Cork, and, greatest of all, Mitchelstown.

At Ardagh Mrs. Dermot O'Brien, the wife of the President of the Royal Hibernian Academy, established her own cheese factory. Another lady owns a cheese dairy on the banks of the Boyne. This is the formula Mrs. O'Brien used for making Ardagh cheese :

Proportion of butter-fat, 3.5.

Use mixed morning's and evening's milk.

Raise to 84 degrees F.

At .21 to .22 per cent. acidity or a 22 second rennet test add rennet to bring about coagulation in 40 minutes. Stir deeply into milk for 3-5 minutes, lightly on surface till it shows signs of coagulating. Leave to set.

When curd shows a " clear split," cut it twice vertically, twice horizontally, leaving 3 minutes between each cut.

Raise slowly to 98 degrees F., stirring all the time, first lightly with hands, then with wooden rake.

Scald about 40 minutes till whey shows .19 or .20 acidity ($\frac{1}{4}$ in hot iron test).

Draw off whey, let curd settle, break up and toss lightly with hands 10-15 minutes. This aeration greatly improves flavour.

Pack in caerphilly moulds and put under light pressure for 20 minutes ; turn out, reverse and put under increased pressure one hour ; turn out, reverse, and put under still increased pressure four hours.

Turn out, trim edges and leave exposed to air (temp. about 50° F.) 12 hours. Reverse and rub all over very thoroughly with salt and leave 12 hours. Reverse, salt again and leave 12 hours. Dip in brine (1 lb. salt to 1 gal. water) and put on ripening shelf. Turn every day for 3-4 weeks when it should be fit for use. It can be kept for 6 months.

I found that the rind of a cheese is obtained by immersing the cheese in salt water.

The next question that interested me was, what is it that causes the difference between cheeses? Why are there holes in Gruyère and why is Gorgonzola foetid? To a great extent it is a matter of temperature, and of the conditions and nature of the milk used—goat's or ewe's. The effervescence of certain gases produce the cavernous cheeses such as Gruyère, and the presence of mites, the odour and "ripeness" of Gorgonzola The nature of the soil on which the dairy is situated is an important factor in giving its character to a cheese.

"The cheese has to be good," Mrs. O'Brien said, "because at Ardagh we are on the limestone." Now the question of the fertility of soils rose in my mind. The most fertile lands are not the best for human life. No country is more fertile in a sense than Brazil, but there the trees are of a better fibre than the men. What is it that constitutes a land's fertility? Fertility, that is, in its relation to human beings. When I motored out from Palermo to Mon Reale, the Sicilian chauffeur became eloquent. Waving his arm towards what looked like a bay raised of old from the sea-bed, he exclaimed, "That is the Concho d'oro. The most fertile land in the world. It grows the olive, the citron, the vine and the corn." "Hold hard!" I exclaimed, "and tell me would it turn a bullock worth £11 into one worth £32 in eleven months without shelter or stall-feeding? No! It would have first to produce turnips to feed the oxen." (This was before our calf-skinning Government emerged.) That of course is the real test of a land's fertility—the power of transubstantiating grass directly into the highest form of protein for human consumption.

Sicelides Musae, paulo maiora canamus,
Non omnis arbusta juvant humilesque myricae.

The limestone land ! The nurse of heroes whether they be men like the men of Sparta, or the artists of Pentelicon, or Derby winners on whole hooves, or bulls with splendid flashing coats or milch cows udder-deep in lush grass. That is why Irish cheese off the bone-forming limestone is better than all the pallid or putrescent shapes of Italy.

Before I print other instructions for cheese-making which have been regulated by modern science I must pay a tribute of

"WHO FIRST LIGHTED ON THE FACT."

astonishment and admiration for our predecessors who arrived by empirical methods at results which, save for the principals of asepsis and standardisation, cannot be outdone by modern means.

Who first lighted on the fact that rennet, the fourth stomach of a calf or a rabbit's stomach or Galium, or " Lady's bed-straw," would curdle milk ? Who, when it was curdled, went on through all the processes required to turn the curd into cheese ? Who first dared to eat it then ? Cheese is one of the discoveries equal almost to the discovery of wine, or beer with which it goes so well. It is as simple and as useful as the

157

discovery that by a system of locks in a canal water could be made to bear a boat uphill. But now rennet is prepared and standardised and distributed in the strengths required to the dairies for the cheeses they produce.

I now quote from a leaflet issued by the Department of Agriculture (Mr. Hogan's department.) It is entitled *Cheese-making on the Farm*. It will explain how cheeses differ and what a " cream " cheese is.

" Cheese forms a most valuable article of diet, as it is rich in proteins or flesh-forming food as well as in fat. Fat and proteins in approximately equal quantities constitute about two-thirds of a good Cheddar cheese. In the manufacture of butter, practically the only constituent taken from the milk is the fat, but in the manufacture of cheese the casein or curd, as well as the fat, is utilised. While it takes about $2\frac{1}{3}$ gallons of milk to produce one pound of butter, one gallon of milk will yield about one pound of cheese." Here I inquired why did any one make any "white meat" out of milk but cheese, seeing that $1\frac{1}{3}$ gallons of milk would be saved. The answer to this is that cheese leaves no buttermilk for calves and for its many uses.

" The manufacture of small cheese for home consumption can be carried out with success on the farm, as, apart from the necessary cheese-moulds, rennet extract and cheese cloths, the apparatus required consists of, or may be improvised from, the utensils usually employed in butter-making.

" Cheese can be made in the dairy and cured in an unused pantry or dry cellar, but any clean and well-ventilated room may be utilised. The temperature of the curing-room influences the ripening of the cheese ; too low or too high a temperature spoils the flavour. The most suitable temperature is 58 degrees F. to 60 degrees F.

" The milk for cheese-making must be pure, clean and free from taints. Defects in this connection are not so easily overcome in the manufacture of cheese as in butter-making.

" For making Cottage Cheese the utensils required are: 2 milk pails (one of about 3 gallons capacity, and the other slightly larger). One tablespoon, 1 teaspoon, 1 thermometer, 1 carving knife, 1 cup, 1 tin disc of about 3 inches diameter, 1 cheese mould capable of holding 2½ to 3 lb cheese (size 6 inches by 4 inches with wooden follower). Weights: 7, 14, 28 and 56 lb, 1 butter board, cheese muslin. These are also required: liquid rennet extract of a recognised dairy brand; salt.

" The milk for cheese-making should be perfectly clean, and may be either mixed night's and morning's or all morning's milk. A gallon of milk will produce about 1 lb of ripe cheese, and a cheese suitable for family use can be made from 2½ gallons.

" The milk (2½ gallons) is carefully strained through muslin into the smaller pail, which is then placed standing in the second pail, containing water at 90 degrees F., or at the temperature necessary to bring the milk to 86 degrees F. Four tablespoonfuls of soured milk or fresh buttermilk are strained and mixed into the milk in order to produce the necessary acidity.

" One teaspoonful of rennet is mixed with ½ cupful of cold water. The diluted rennet thus prepared is carefully stirred into the milk for 3 minutes, after which the surface of the milk is gently agitated until coagulation commences. The milk pail is then covered with the muslin cloth and left until the curd is firm enough to cut. The curd is cut when it splits with a clean fracture over an inserted finger, generally 50 to 60 minutes from the time of adding the rennet.

" At this point the muslin cloth is removed, and the curd is first cut into ½-inch squares by means of the carving knife, and then into ½-inch cubes by using the tin disc in a circular sloping movement.

" The curd is next gently stirred for 30 minutes, the temperature being raised at the same time to 98 degrees F. by pouring water at 110 degrees F. into the outer pail. The curd is allowed to settle at this temperature for 30 minutes, but in order to prevent the particles of curd from adhering together, it is stirred up for 2 minutes at 10-minute intervals.

" The curd and whey are now covered and allowed to remain undisturbed for 30 minutes. At the end of this time as much of the whey as possible is ladled from the curd, which is then poured into a muslin cloth tied over the top of the second pail. This done, the cloth containing the curd is taken by three corners in the left hand and the fourth corner is wrapped round so that any superfluous moisture is forced from the curd.

" Following this operation the bundle of curd is placed on the butter-board and opened out, the curd is loosely broken and separated, and 1 tablespoonful of salt is well mixed in until all the salt is dissolved.

" The cheese mould is lined with damp muslin, and the curd carefully packed into the mould. The ends of the muslin are folded over the top, the follower is placed in position and a 7-lb weight is laid on the follower.

" After half an hour the cheese is taken out, turned in the cloth, and put back to press under a pressure of 14 lbs. This pressure is increased to 28 lbs in about 2 hours time, and the cheese is left until the following morning, when it is taken out, turned into a dry muslin and returned to press under 56 lbs pressure for about 2 hours.

" The cheese is next taken out, carefully greased with lard or butter and placed for ripening on a clean shelf in an airy room, free from draughts, at a temperature of from 58 degrees to 60 degrees F. During this ripening process the cheese should be turned every day for three weeks, at the end of which time it should be sufficiently ripe for home consumption."

CREAM CHEESE

" This popular cheese, of which there are two varieties, viz., the renneted or single cream cheese, and the unrenneted or double cream cheese, is very easy to make.

"The utensils necessary are :—2 pudding basins (3 pint size), 1 egg-cup, 1 dinner knife, 1 butter or fruit knife, 1 tea-spoon, 1 tablespoon, 1 huckaback towel, 2 large plates, 1 2-lb weight, 1 thermometer, 1 cheese mould $2\frac{1}{2}$" $\times$ 2" $\times$ 1" high (a patty pan will serve the purpose). Also required :—Liquid rennet extract of a recognised dairy brand. Salt."

SINGLE CREAM CHEESE

" The cream for single cream cheese should always be as fresh as possible. If it is necessary to use hand-skimmed cream, the morning milk should be ' set ' and skimmed for the cheese in the evening. A little clean soured milk or buttermilk is mixed with the cream before the rennet is added, to produce the necessary acidity. One pint of thin cream (containing about 20 per cent of fat) will make two cheeses weighing about $\frac{1}{4}$lb each.

" The cream (1 pint) is placed in one of the basins and brought to a temperature of from 60 degrees to 65 degrees F. One teaspoonful of soured milk is mixed with the cream. Four drops of rennet extract (mixed with a teaspoonful of cold water in an egg-cup) are gently stirred into the cream for 3 minutes, and the basin is covered with the towel about twelve hours in a well-ventilated room, free from all draughts and at a temperature of 60 degrees F.

" The second basin is then lined with the towel and the coagulated cream having been cut into 2-inch squares with the dinner knife, is, by means of the tablespoon, ladled into the cloth lining the basin. The curd in the cloth is tied into a bundle, which is hung up in a draught and left to drain. The cloth is opened out about every two hours, and the curd scraped from it and mixed, the butter knife being used for the purpose. A pinch of salt is mixed with the curd at the last scraping at night in order to prevent it from becoming too acid.

" The following morning the curd is again scraped from the cloth, mixed and hung up for about two hours, when it should be fairly firm. The cloth is next untied, and the corners are folded round the curd which is now put to press between two plates (the top one being inverted) for about two hours, under a pressure of about two pounds. The cheese is then ready to mould ; a patty pan, lined with muslin, serves excellently for this purpose. The cheese is pressed into the mould with the butter knife ; when the mould is full it is inverted and the cheese turned out. A little additional salt may, if desired, be mixed with the cheese before it is moulded.

" Cream cheese should be perfectly smooth in texture and about as firm as fresh butter. It may be eaten when quite fresh, or kept for a few days to allow the flavour to develop. It should not, however, be kept for more than a week."

UNRENNETED OR DOUBLE CREAM CHEESE

" The cream used for making double cream cheese should contain 50 per cent to 60 per cent of fat.

" One pint of thick cream from the separator is placed in a pudding basin and cooled to 60 degrees F. A teaspoonful of clean soured milk is strained into the cream, which is then well mixed, covered with the towel, and placed on a shelf for 12 hours in an airy room free from draughts. The cream is then ladled with the tablespoon into the dry towel lining the second basin. The cloth is tied into a bundle, hung up to drain, and afterwards treated according to the foregoing directions for the manufacture of single cream cheese."

BONDON CHEESE

"This is a soft cheese usually made from a mixture of whole and separated milk or buttermilk, or from partly skimmed milk.

" It may also be made from whole milk, in which case the finished product is much richer than Bondon cheese made from partly skimmed milk. For its manufacture in small quantities the following utensils are required :—

"2 pudding basins (2½-3 pint size), 1 egg-cup, 1 dinner knife, 1 butter or fruit knife, 1 teaspoon, 1 tablespoon, 1 huckaback towel, 2 large plates, 1 2-lb weight, 1 thermometer, 1 cheese mould, 2¾ inches diameter and 2½ inches high (a patty pan will serve the purpose), 1 straw mat. Also required :—Liquid rennet extract of a recognised dairy brand. Salt.

" When the whole milk is used, 1 quart is placed in a basin, and 2 tablespoonfuls of clean soured milk are strained and mixed into it. When partly skimmed milk is used, the proprotion of skim or separated milk should not exceed 6 tablespoonfuls to every quart of new milk. Buttermilk may also be substituted, but in this case no other starter is required. The temperature of the mixture is brought from 60 degrees to 65 degrees F. Four drops of liquid rennet extract diluted in a little cold water are well mixed into the milk. The vessel containing the milk is covered with the towel and placed on a shelf for 12 hours in a well-ventilated room at a temperature of from 60 degrees to 65 degrees F.

" A dinner knife is then taken and the curd cut into 2-inch squares. The second basin having been lined with the dry towel, the curd is ladled in very thin layer into the cloth, the tablespoon being used for the purpose. The corners of the towel are tied in a knot, and the bundle is hung up to drain. The cloth is opened out about every two hours and the curd (by means of the butter knife) scraped from it and mixed. A pinch of salt is mixed with the curd at the last scraping at night in order to prevent it from becoming too acid.

" The following morning the curd is again scraped from the cloth, mixed and hung up for about two hours, after which time it should be fairly firm. The cloth is next untied, and the corners are folded round the curd, which is put to press between two plates (the top one inverted) for about two hours under a pressure of two pounds.

" At this stage the cheese is ready to mould. A little salt may, if desired, be mixed into it before it is moulded. The mould is placed over the straw mat (which should have been previously scalded) and the cheese tightly pressed into it. When the cheese is firm enough to retain its shape, which should be in about an hour's time, it may be removed from the mould.

" Bondon cheese may be eaten fresh, or it may be kept on the straw mats and turned daily for a period of from eight to ten days. When thus kept it develops a distinctive flavour.

" This year the production of cheese in the dairies of Ireland has increased. More cheese is being used *pace* George Moore by the Irish themselves ; but much more is being exported to England. This is auspicious for an improvement in relations between the two countries. Instead of a rivalry

OLD FARMHOUSE OR MASS PRODUCTION.

between the dairy farmers—for there is no limit to the English market—an approachment between those who produce the same food is surely to be expected. I have referred to the peaceful and almost soporific effect of cheese on the consumer. This is the greatest argument I can think of and I offer it in its favour. Let us share a meal round a common board, eat more cheese, a double cheese, one of those 'suitable for family use' for preference, and together hum ' Bethankit! ' "

XII.

BLUE VINNY

XII.—BLUE VINNY

By André L. Simon

Blue Vinny is a hard cheese and a rare cheese made in Dorset and nowhere else. It is made of skimmed milk and it is as white as chalk with a deep royal blue vein right through. There are ever so many other hard cheeses made of skimmed milk, but none can boast anything like the same " Cordon Bleu " which is the pride and the distinctive mark of the true Blue Vinny.

Let us first of all consider the nature of hard cheeses and their making before looking for the reason why. Blue Vinny is not only blue but rare.

Milk is mostly water : even the best milk contains some 80 per cent. of water before any milkman has even looked at it. But this large quantity of water in milk, important as it is, has merely the importance of the canvas upon which the picture is painted. There would have been no picture had there been no canvas, but what we look at and enjoy are the very small quantities of a large number of colour pigments spread on the canvas by the hand of the artist. In milk there are also a large number of different pigments wonderfully arranged by the greatest of all artists—Nature. There is fat, the milk fat which is more commonly known as butter fat ; there are proteins such as lactalbumin, casein, globulin and others ; there are carbohydrates, chiefly lactose ; there are organic acids, most important of all lactic acid, but small quantities of citric acid and minute quantities of acetic acid ;

there are also traces of all sorts of strange organic substances, not strange in themselves but strange to find in such company ; urea and alcohol, for instance, lecithin, creatinine, hypoxanthin and lactochrome. And even now we have not come to the end of the truly extraordinary list of all that men of science have discovered in milk. There are also in milk minute yet most important quantities of mineral salts of sodium, potassium, calcium, magnesium and iron, and, finally, some enzymes and vitamins.

Milk is by no manner of means a standard article. There are all sorts and conditions of milk, and the proportion of fats to acids, as well as the presence or absence of some of the minor substances just mentioned, depends upon a number of different factors. The first is the species or breed of the milk-giver : cow, ass, goat or ewe. The second is the condition of the milk-giver : its state of health, the quantity and quality of its feed, whether grazed in the open, in the summer, or fed indoors on patent " cake " during the winter months. These are initial differences : they are responsible for milk making a good, bad or indifferent start in the race, but there is a long course in front of it and many hurdles before the winning post is reached, the winning post being, in our case, a perfect Blue Vinny cheese.

The moment milk leaves the cow its troubles begin : they are mostly internal troubles. Milk is unstable. It is made up of so many different substances that differences are inevitable among them. What is best in milk is what is fattest, a consoling thought for some of us. Still more encouraging is the fact that what is fattest and best in milk is also the lightest, so that it soon comes to the surface, where the farmer's wife has no difficulty in taking it away in the form and by the name of cream, leaving in the pail no longer whole milk but

" skimmed " milk, the sort of milk which is wanted to make Blue Vinny cheese.

When it has been robbed of its cream, milk is more unstable than ever and it is very much inclined to prove its annoyance by turning sour, which men of science explain by telling us that what sugar there is in milk turns to lactic acid. Something drastic has to be done and something really drastic is done. *Rennet* is introduced to the " slenderised " or skimmed milk. Rennet is a strange creature, known as an unorganised ferment, a curious substance which nobody can make nor explain, but one that is found in the gastric juice of all mammals at the time when they are suckling their young. So before we can hope that our milk will even begin to think of becoming Blue Vinny, we have—or somebody has—to go and get rennet where rennet is usually found, and that is in the fourth stomach, or vell, of calves. How much rennet we shall put in our milk depends upon the temperature at the time, and the quantity of milk, but a little goes a long way, from three to five ounces are ample for one hundred gallons of milk.

The moment rennet is put into milk, a great storm rages within and the milk positively goes to pieces—pieces of *curd*. There is in rennet a curious chemical substance called *rennin* which is responsible for the coagulation and precipitation, in the form of curd, of the casein present in milk both in partial solution and in combination with the lime there is in milk. *Curd* is a combination of para-casein with lime and calcium phosphates. It holds and keeps safely and freely most of the fat globules in milk. It is the first step from sick or rather unstable milk towards sound and more stable cheese.

What makes rennet so remarkable is that it does its appointed job of work in a wonderfully efficient manner, thanks to the

171

perfect team work of its two partners : *rennin* and *pepsin,* both holding equal shares in the rennet firm, but different functions. Rennet having produced the curd, its work is done. Pepsin's work only begins then and its task shall not end until the day when we shall eat our Blue Vinny. Pepsin's first work is to digest the curd itself and, later, when the curd has become cheese, pepsin still stands by to make cheese digestible. It sounds simple enough, but in real life—or merely cheese life—all sorts of difficulties and complications are always sure to crop up. Rennin, for instance, is unreasonably susceptible to variations of temperature and pepsin to the presence or absence of acids. There is a close connection between these two partners : the pepsin, the one appointed to finish the job, cannot do it satisfactorily unless the rennin, the curd-maker, has done its part of the work neither too hurriedly nor too leisurely. That depends entirely upon the temperature at the time of renneting. Rennin acts best at a temperature of 105° Fahr., but such a temperature is not practical in cheese-making, since it would result in curd far too firm for the making of good cheese. In the case of Blue Vinny, temperatures from 80° to 90° Fahr. at renneting time are best. When the temperature is too high, the curd becomes firm much more rapidly, so much so that it does not absorb and in-corporate a sufficient proportion of acids. On the contrary, should the temperature be too low, the action of the rennin will be retarded : it will take much longer to get together and that will be firm enough for milling, and that curd will be too acid. Pepsin cannot deal with any degree of satisfaction with non-acid curd and it will digest far too rapidly over-acid curd. Hence the importance of regulating the temperature at the time of renneting, so that rennin may hand over its partner pepsin, the right kind of curd to be made into good cheese.

172

When we have secured our curd of the right consistency and acidity, we may consider ourselves fortunate in having cleared the first hurdle. The next step consists in putting the curd through the curd-mill. This is done to squeeze out of the curd as much as possible of the watery whey still left in it. When taken out the mill, the curd should have a smooth, velvety feel and its flavour should be as sweet as the flavour of ripe cream. It is then broken up and salted, the salt not being added to assist the pepsin but merely for the sake of palatability. The milled and salted curd is then put in a chesset or cheese press ; it is pressed, turned over and pressed again and again in order to get out as much of the water that may still be there.

When it comes out of the chesset, curd is curd no longer, but Cheese ; cheese, but not yet Blue Vinny. It is usual to give it a bath, that is to plunge it in very hot water for a short time in order to harden the outside rind-to-be. After its bath, it is greased and all that remains to be done is to leave it high and dry in a well-ventilated room, there to settle down, mature and grow *Blue*.

But the time has come for us to journey to the West and have a look at the country of the Blue Vinny.

The County of Dorset is not one of the largest, but it is one of the most charming in England because of the variety and beauty of its landscape. Not so beautiful but most illuminating is the geological map of Dorset ; every shade of browns and greens so dear to the cartographer are mixed in the most hopeless looking sort of Chinese puzzle : there are samples of all manner of rocks ; there are stretches of sandy soil, seams of white lime, plenty of cold clay and a sprinkling of rich loam valleys. "What has it to do with Blue Vinny, anyhow ? " the impatient reader might possibly be inclined to ask. The answer is " Everything." The quality of the cheese depends upon the quality of the milk in the first place. The quality of the milk depends chiefly upon the quality of the grass available for the cattle, and the quality of the grass depends mostly upon the soil and subsoil of the land. The more sandy the soil, the better the grass for sheep and the worse for cattle. That is why they have never yet, nor will they ever make decent cheese in Suffolk : the soil is too light.

> Cheese such as men in Suffolk make
> But wished it Stilton for his sake.
> (Pope—*Imitations of Horace* Sat. VI. I. ii.)

Long before the reign of Queen Anne, not only was Suffolk cheese unpopular but the servants question was already troublesome :

". . . and so home, where I found my wife vexed at her people for grumbling to eat Suffolk cheese, which I also am vexed at. So to bed." (Pepys. Oct. 4, 1661.)

Suffolk is all sandy soil and there is no hope for Suffolk, no cheese hope. Dorset is only partly sand, hence its ability to produce both tender mutton and Blue Vinny. The sheep and cattle pastures of Dorset are scattered over the face of the County according to the multi-coloured geological map and the quality of the milk varies very appreciably according to the nature of the grazing grounds. Why should it be so ? Simply because the roots of the grass do not get from the soil merely moisture but infinitesimal quantities of various mineral salts which make all the difference to the texture and flavour of the grass in the first place and of the milk and its cheese later. This is the reason why Blue Vinny has always been a rare cheese and always will be. It can only be made from the milk of a very

" MY WIFE VEXED AT HER PEOPLE GRUMBLING TO EAT SUFFOCK CHEESE
. . . AND SO TO BED."

limited number of herds, those privileged to enjoy the rich
pasture lands in the immediate vicinity of Sherborne, and only
during the summer months, when the grazing is at its best,
and also the milk. There is a further factor of scarcity in the
fact that not all the cheese made from the best milk, from the
best herds and at the best time of the year, will necessarily
show any " blue." Most of them, nowadays, and more of them
every year, remain as white as chalk without the faintest
tracing of either blue or any other colour. That is the great
mystery—Nature's own secret—about Blue Vinny. The blue in
it is not painted on nor put in by anybody. It has to come in of

its own accord and there is no really satisfactory explanation of how it comes or refuses to come. All that is known is that the blue of Blue Vinny is due to a mould. But what is a mould? A mould is one of the most mysterious—because still so imperfectly understood—forms of life. The air we breathe and the world we live in are packed full of all sorts of moulds which we do not see, any more than we hear all the tunes which are broadcast from all the stations of the earth, which cross and recross each other's paths and yet retain their own identity and are available to all who know how to capture them. Moulds can also be identified and looked at under powerful microscopes. They can be separated and made to grow to such an extent that everybody can see them with the naked eye. Moulds belong to the large family of the fungi. They are vegetative bodies with an outer coat known as " Exospore," and an inner coat known as " Endospore." They grow through an interconnected series of tubular structures known as " Hyphae," and their growth is affected, assisted or checked, by a number of stimuli such as light, gravity, oxygen, etc. Like all members of that disreputable family of fungi, moulds are parasitic in their habits. Their " Hyphae " absorb food through the tissues or walls of their slender tubes, and these slowly but surely penetrate farther and farther into the very substance of their hosts, producing lateral shoots capable of absorbing sufficient food material to give birth to a number of similar threads which become knotted or woven together into a sort of cord or line or else keep apart and permeate the whole of the body of the host. The host, in this case being the cheese, the mould of a roaming disposition will produce Stilton or Gorgonzola whilst the far rarer mould of more regular working, the one that keeps to a straight course and ties itself in a knot, produces the curious markings of the Blue Vinny.

But the blue of the Blue Vinny or of any other cheese, is no Mouldy Mucor. It is cheese, but cheese affected by the catalytic action of a mould. A mould is a catalyst. What is a catalyst? A catalyst is a remover of hindrances. It does not actually do any work at all, but it removes the obstacle that was in the way of the worker. A drop of oil does not make the wheels go round; it does not push them on, but it removes the friction that would have made them stop. The electric switch might be called a catalyst in the sense that the electric power is powerless to bridge the break which the switch will repair, making possible the passage of the current. In a much more complicated manner, although the basic principle is the same, all sorts of parasitic fungi act as catalysts. Their "Hyphae" consist of protoplasm and nuclei, and they may also contain, like other vegetable cells, infinitesimal, but very important, quantities of various substances, such as crystals of calcium oxalate and others which are responsible for the distinctive colouring of different cheeses. And quite distinct from this the most apparent although the least important of the parasite's action upon its host, the "Hyphae" of the mould, as they grow, excrete a certain "Enzyme" which render possible all sorts of molecular readjustments of the substances which come in contact with it. This is the catalytic action which in everyday parlance means that your cheese has a chance of maturing as it should.

Why should the blue of the Blue Vinny be different from the veining or "moulding" of other cheeses? Because the original mucor or mould is different. It is just the same with the yeast that is natural to different vineyards. When the grapes are ripe, there appears upon their skins, as upon the skin of all fruit grown out of doors, a very fine grey down. It consists of millions of microscopic fungi which are in the air and in the soil of the vineyards but cannot get a hold upon the grape skins until the grapes when nearing their ripe stage the skin becomes softer. When the grapes are pressed, these fungi get at the sugar of the grape juice and thrive upon it ; they grow so fast that their Enzyme soon upsets the balance of the grape juice in such a way that the whole of the grape sugar disappears and is replaced by ethylic alcohol and carbonic acid gas. This phenomenon, known as fermentation, is constant, but the yeast which is responsible for it varies with the species of grapes and the soil of the vineyards where the grapes are grown, and the differences between the bouquet and savour of different wines are in a great measure due to differences in the yeasts. It is the same with the various moulds ; the actual mechanism of their action may—nay, must—be the same, but different results are nevertheless achieved owing to differences of origin. That is to say that the white downy mucor that grows upon some derelict carrots, for instance, are not identical to the white downy mucor upon some cast-off boot, although both will not only look the same but behave in the same manner if introduced into two identical newly made cheeses. This is why no Blue Vinny will ever be made anywhere else but in Dorset, if it is made at all in a few years' time.

Although Blue Vinny is a hard cheese made from skimmed milk, there is a very great difference between milk skimmed by the farmer's wife who has just removed the thick cream from the top, and the milk treated by the brutal separator and robbed of all its goodness. However good the milk might have been to start with, there is so much taken out of it by the mechanical separator that no cheese made from what liquid is left can ever be of real goodness. To have tasted of a " Best " Blue Vinny made of whole milk by a well-to-do farmer for himself or a very special friend, is to be spoilt for ever

"MOULDY OLD BOOTS OR STRAPS OR LEATHER."

more, not only for the average skimmed milk Blue Vinny but for the best Stilton. The average Stilton is infinitely superior to the average chalky Blue Vinny, but even this average Blue Vinny is getting rarer every year. Every year the proportion of Blue Vinny Cheeses that are "Blue" is smaller compared to the number of so-called Blue Dorset Cheeses which are entirely white. There seems to be something wrong with the spores of mould which no longer turn the cheese blue. As a matter of fact, there is nothing that can rightly be called wrong, since greater cleanliness must surely be right and it is most probably because of the use of antiseptics and generally speaking the greater care in the scrubbing and washing of dairies that the Blue Vinny is no longer blue. Old farmers will tell you that the set of old harness in some odd corner or upon a rafter, a set derelict for years and covered with thick white mould, has never been rubbed nor thrown away because his father before him had an idea that mouldy old boots or straps or leather of any kind was always to be somewhere about if the cheese was to turn the right blue. It may be just one of those curious coincidences without any foundation in fact, or it may be due to some unascertained yet ascertainable scientific connection between moulds and leather. The matter might have been given far more searching attention at the hands of investigators duly qualified to elucidate the causation of the blue in Blue Vinny, had this been the only cheese in England, or even one of the main pillars of the Cheese industry, such as Cheddar. But it is not. Blue Vinny has never been more than a locally famous cheese, in the first place because there has never been enough of it to go round the London Cheese Markets, let alone the markets of the whole country. In the second place, because the average Blue Vinny is not at all the sort of Cheese that will raise any measure of true enthusiasm. It is a dull cheese. A welcome change once in a way, but not an everyday cheese, a stand-by cheese like Stilton, Cheshire or Cheddar.

At any of the big London stores, when one asks for Blue Vinny, the answer is the same : they have not had any for ever so long. But they know the name. The name will probably survive the cheese itself, and there may be some people who wonder what is the meaning of this name or where it comes from.

All the cheese made in Dorsetshire is not Vinny. There is a cheese they call Rammil, Rammel or Rammilk, which is made from the Raw Milk, the whole of the milk, cream and all, whilst Vinny always was the cheese made from milk from which the cream had been taken away as it rose to the top. This skimmed milk cheese is the cheese known as Blue Dorset, or else Blue Vinny, and formerly Blue Vinid.

But why Vinny or Vinid? Because of the " Blue " mouldiness of the Cheese. *Vinewed* is an old West Country word which means " mouldy," and as the old West of England people pronounce " sinew " " sinney," so they also pronounce " vinew," meaning 'mould,' " vinney," hence Vinny. In the same way, " vinewed," meaning 'mouldy,' became " vinew," meaning 'mould,' " vinney," hence Vinny. In the same way, " vinewed," meaning 'mouldy,' became " vineyed " or " vinid." In Richardson's Dictionary, " Vinny " or " Vinewed " is derived from Fynig, the past participle of the Anglo-Saxon Fynig-Ean, meaning to spoil, corrupt or decay. Richardson adds :

" Lye remarks that the Devonshire people call bread, cheese, etc., Vinny, when spoilt by mould or must."